D0408481

Out of the Frying Pan

Out of the Frying Pan

A CHEF'S MEMOIR OF
HOT KITCHENS, SINGLE MOTHERHOOD,
AND THE FAMILY MEAL

GILLIAN CLARK

THOMAS DUNNE BOOKS
ST. MARTIN'S PRESS 🐟 NEW YORK

The events in this book are as true as I remember them. Some of the names have been changed. Everything else is as it happened.

THOMAS DUNNE BOOKS.
An imprint of St. Martin's Press.

OUT OF THE FRYING PAN. Copyright © 2007 by Gillian Clark.
All rights reserved. Printed in the United States of America.
No part of this book may be used or reproduced in any manner
whatsoever without written permission except in the case of
brief quotations embodied in critical articles or reviews.
For information, address St. Martin's Press, 175 Fifth Avenue,
New York, N.Y. 10010.

www.thomasdunnebooks.com
www.stmartins.com

Book design by Gretchen Achilles

Library of Congress Cataloging-in-Publication Data

Clark, Gillian, 1963–
    Out of the frying pan : a chef's memoir of hot kitchens, single
motherhood, and the family meal / Gillian Clark. — 1st ed.
        p. cm.
    ISBN-13: 978-0-312-36693-3
    ISBN-10: 0-312-36693-0
    1. Clark, Gillian, 1962– 2. Cooks—Washington (D.C.)—Biog-
raphy. 3. Colorado Kitchen (Washington, D.C.) 4. Cookery,
American. I. Title.
    TX649.C57A3 2007
    641.5092—dc22
    [B]
                                                    2007022283

First Edition: October 2007

10 9 8 7 6 5 4 3 2 1

To my family—those with whom I shared a kitchen
and those with whom I share DNA.
The bonds formed making meals together and having meals together are
stronger than I ever imagined. I've come to realize that not just blood,
but also cooking oil, is thicker than water.

Acknowledgments

Thanks to everyone who taught me to cook (in order of appearance): my mother, my father, Aunt Daisy, Nana, Ms. Cotrazola, Craig Claiborne, Magalee, François, Pascal, Alain Lecomte, Susan Lindeborg, Ann Cashion, Sian, and Robin Smith.

Table of Contents

CONTENTS

The Recipes

THE RECIPES

Out of the Frying Pan

Prologue

LIGHTING THE PILOT

Our minivan came to a shaking halt in the Virginia mud, miles from any paved road and a world away from the one-way streets and parking meters of our home in Washington, DC. When my family and I tumbled out, we found ourselves beside an old barn shedding red paint like a roasted pepper flaking off shards of crisped skin. A low stone wall crumbled beside what was the foundation of a house that had burned down twenty years ago. It was four acres of a two-hundred-acre farm for sale.

As we all stood in the grassy center of what I had already started calling *our farm*, I breathed in the smell of the place. It was crisp and earthy with a slightly sharp edge of burning wood and the sweet smell of rotting leaves. I felt my soul settling in. Here was the peace and calm I'd been searching for. In a matter of months this could be ours.

The farmer had harvested the last of the soybean and winter wheat and was selling the family farm in pieces. This little corner where tall grass mingled with stray stalks of wheat was all that was left. The charred remains of the old split-level made this last parcel a hard sell. The owner had lowered the price by twenty thousand dollars and I had raised my hopes—maybe it could be done. I could merge my dream of having a career in food with my need to be with my family. First, I had to get my husband and two young daughters to see what I was seeing.

The key was to make this open plot of land look like home. The farm was real and within our grasp and just the thing we needed. Sure, it was my specific dream to raise fatted geese and other game birds, but couldn't we all find some of what we were looking for?

We followed the red-flagged stakes that marked the perimeter of what would be *our* farm. I took a stone from the creek to mark where our front door would be. I promised five-year-old Magalee that she could help paint the barn, which would be just fine for equipment, I told her, but the geese would need bigger and more modern accommodations. I showed Sian, who was just two, how she could stand amid the always hungry quail and scatter corn to them.

"Honey, a place in Virginia would cut your commute." For my husband, now ending his day with a little too much beer to salve his ever-growing dissatisfaction with his job, the farm represented an important change. When things got off the ground, it would be a chance for him to do the work with his hands—the real engineering—he had talked so much about.

They all began to see how this could be the perfect home for us. Standing in that field in front of the old barn with its rusted tin roof and splintered doors, I felt as if the last puzzle piece had just snapped into place.

I knew I needed a life change. I was still living on antacids. I had thought that leaving a stressful office job to start my own promotional consulting firm would be a relief—my best chance to get away from the creativity-stifling office politics that were churning the acids in my stomach. But the only difference was that I worked from home and was just a few feet from my kitchen at all times. When three big gulps from the pale blue bottle didn't dissolve the stress from a day of writing copy or launching a sales brochure, I found solace at the stove.

Simmering shallots in butter while white wine steamed to reduction made my kitchen feel like a sauna. It often followed that the more stressed I was, the more elaborate the meal I'd prepare. Stuffed shoulder of veal with sherry and shiitakes followed the frantic call from a client wanting to change a brochure that was printed, folded, and ready to mail. Corn-crusted scallops with apple brandy sauce came after the proposal, which took sixteen hours to complete, received no response from the anxious start-up. Then there were the times when, for no reason in particular, I dug through stacks of clipped recipes and scrawled notes to attempt the perfect roast chicken.

Cooking was the only thing that gave me that elusive feeling of accomplishment. It relaxed me. It was more soothing than four or five fire-quenching swigs of antacid. When I cooked I could see what was often not so clear in marketing communications. The clean plates after dinner told me all I needed to know. There was no wondering and waiting. No anxiety, just immediate gratification. Something marketing—even from home—was failing to give me. The more I thought about it, the more I was convinced that I could make a living doing what I enjoy. If I didn't answer this call, I'd regret it.

•   •   •

By the time we'd visited the farm, I'd already saved up enough to pay for cooking school, finished up the last projects and closed my company, and begun school. I had turned my back on marketing for good.

In a clean chef coat I sat in class on the edge of my seat. The Practique classroom at L'Académie de Cuisine was much like my high-school chemistry lab except for the huge Vulcan stove against the wall by the room's only window. At the lab tables would be little Cassette-Feu stoves (single-burner stoves fueled with butane), or standing mixers, or sometimes pasta machines. There were about twelve rows of these lab tables surrounded by uncomfortable wooden stools, making sitting for long stretches nearly impossible. Up front Chef Pascal would be at the chalkboard drawing the primal cuts of veal or writing down the recipe for dacquoise, a complicated, classic French dessert. I hung on every word. I pulled the strings of my apron tight around my waist the same way Pascal did. Downstairs during Chef François's lectures on theory, I absorbed the principles of sauce making and wine pairing like a sponge. I had never been a great student, but now I was at the top of my class.

Then talk of working in the business seeped into the lectures. It was clear that they expected us to work in a restaurant when we left school, and that's when the doubts started to creep up on me. I started thinking that I'd made the biggest mistake of my midlife crisis.

I had a mortgage to pay and day care to consider. As much as I loved the fantasy of working in and, eventually, running a kitchen, I just didn't think I could do it and help support my family at the same time. As unrealistic as it was, I needed to start at the top, where I could set my own schedule and call the shots. Long hours at a low hourly wage in a kitchen meant more dues than I was willing or able to pay.

Then I saw the fatted geese of Gascony.

François was hoping to spark interest in the school's annual trip to France, and it worked. But, while the rest of the class "ooohed" and "aaahed" over the rolling hills and exquisite scenery flashing on the screen from François's slides of the previous year's trip, I was solely interested in those Gascony farms where farmers overfed fat geese so that their little livers swelled into one-and-a-half-pound lobes of foie gras. The geese obediently waddled over to tubes that filled them with greater and greater quantities of food. In no time at all, these fatted geese were walking around with that miracle of liver turned to butter in their bellies.

There was no way I was going to start a grueling career as a line cook in the hope that one distant day, if I were lucky, I'd make it to chef. It took several months of cooking school for me to see that. In my early thirties, I was one of the oldest in my class. With two young children and a husband who would start to hate my new job as he sat alone night after night, my cooking for a living was out of the question. A farm was the answer. I could satisfy this need to be in the food business and at the same time be the kind of wife and mother I'd only read about.

As school wrapped up, I didn't share my classmates' anxiety over leaving the security of the classroom. Like many of them,

I had taken a job at a restaurant in the heart of Virginia wine country, but for me it was to get to know some of the local chefs near what would be our farm. My classmates worried about suffering under a mean, ego-crushing chef in the heat of a high-pressure kitchen while I was contemplating how to store hay and buy feed. I wasn't without concerns, but things seemed to be going smoothly.

I came home from one of the last classes one Tuesday and found the house too quiet. On the coffee table was a six-pack of beer. The cans were still held together by the plastic, but they were empty. There was one just like it in the kitchen. I kicked a third empty six-pack at the top of the stairs.

"What are you doing?" I asked when I entered the bedroom and saw my husband sprawled out on the bed. Hakim had been leaving for work later and later these days. It was apparent to me that on this day, he never left the house for his job at the engineering firm. Instead he had only made it as far as the corner liquor store.

He sat up a little. He had moved on to malt liquor and was raising the can to take another drink. I could tell by the way his upper lip was groping for the opening like an anteater that his head was feeling heavy.

"Why does everyone get to do what they want?" he drawled before letting his head fall back onto the pillows. The conversation didn't improve much when the cans had been thrown away. After he told me he had never wanted any of this, my soon-to-be ex-husband packed and moved back to his parents' house in New York.

I spent a couple of hours staring at a spot on the wall and confessed to myself that I'd been blinded. While I had made plans for the farm, there had been empty bottles in the closet, and jugs of wine for cooking that were suddenly gone.

Without my husband's signature on the loan agreement, my contract was worthless. Another family relocated from the big city and bought our farm. For months after, the girls would often ask me about fatted geese and quail. "Someday," I'd tell them. My dreams would have to be put on hold.

I was now a cook earning minimum wage. With my divorce pending, I was also suddenly a single mother receiving no financial support from an unemployed ex-husband in an addiction-treatment program. I made a halfhearted attempt to return to marketing. I answered a few employment ads, but while waiting for a prospective boss to read over my resume, I recalled what made me run screaming from jobs like this in the first place. If I did get the interview I knew I would be sitting nervously in a stuffy office hoping the things that shouldn't matter—skin color, sex, marital status, age—didn't matter. I wanted nothing more than to be back in a kitchen. I had to make the food business work.

With no husband or geese to fall back on, I was left to basically sink or swim in my stiff new checked pants and chef coat. I had no choice but to succeed. Not being good at this second career meant starving.

It has been more than ten years since I held Magalee's hand and the three of us, with Sian wrapped around my left leg, stepped cautiously out of the old barn of that Virginia farm. Back then there was no way to know that nothing would go as planned. I chased a dream and ended up a single mother faced with less time and considerably less money to raise my children. And there I was at the bottom of the ladder in a business dominated by younger, childless, unfettered go-getters and cutthroats.

Unfortunately, there's no instruction book for this kind of thing. What I found, however—as trial and error took me through single motherhood, and trial by fire advanced me to chef of my own restaurant—was that the lines blurred. Single-handedly managing a household and a commercial kitchen required similar skills. Was I chef to my children and mother to my kitchen staff? It certainly seemed that way sometimes, and not just because food played a major role in both houses. Both jobs required creativity, passion, and imagination. Those weren't an easy ten years. There were times I thought I'd never make it. I couldn't imagine that the girls would grow and the kitchen would calm, but they did, eventually. With a moment to catch my breath, I realized that being a chef and being a mother helped me to become better at both.

CORN-CRUSTED SCALLOPS
WITH APPLE BRANDY SAUCE

When I first made this, the whole family—husbands, wives, in-laws, and grandchildren—were spending Thanksgiving weekend together in the country. It is the kind of elegant first course that has everyone in the room suggesting that you should cook for a living.

MAKES 4 APPETIZER SERVINGS

½ CUP FLOUR

½ CUP CORNMEAL

2 TEASPOONS SALT

1 TEASPOON FRESHLY GROUND BLACK PEPPER

4 EGGS, WELL BEATEN

16 LARGE SCALLOPS (REFRIGERATE OUT OF THE PACKAGE ON TOWELS TO ABSORB AS MUCH LIQUID AS POSSIBLE)

¼ CUP VEGETABLE OIL

4 TEASPOONS BUTTER

3 GRANNY SMITH APPLES, PEELED, CORED, AND THINLY SLICED

½ CUP CHICKEN STOCK

¼ CUP CALVADOS (OR APPLE BRANDY)

Combine half of the flour with the cornmeal, salt, and pepper. Set aside. Add a pinch of salt to the beaten eggs. Add a pinch of salt and pepper to the other ¼ cup of flour. Coat each scallop in the seasoned flour. Then coat with the beaten eggs. Let the excess egg drip off before coating the scallops very well in the cornmeal-flour mixture.

Heat the vegetable oil with 1 teaspoon of butter in a heavy-bottomed sauté pan over medium heat. When the sizzling of the butter begins to die down, add the scallops to the hot oil in a single layer. Turn after 2 minutes, when the scallops have started to brown, and cook for another minute. Remove each scallop carefully from the pan and set it aside on a warm platter. Keep them warm in an oven set at 150 degrees.

Wipe out the sauté pan with a paper towel and add a teaspoon of butter. Add the apple slices. Toss until they are softened and barely brown or caramelized. Remove the apple slices and fan on four plates. Put these plates into the oven. While the pan is still on the heat, pour the stock into it and turn the heat to high. Bring the stock to a boil and reduce to one-third of its original volume. Add the Calvados and simmer until it is reduced by half and slightly thickened. Whisk in the remaining 2 teaspoons of butter. Pour the sauce over the apple slices, and then arrange the scallops on the plates, over the apples and sauce. Serve immediately.

One

They say the experience of your first cooking job never leaves you. Outside of the culinary school sanctuary is where the real learning begins. In the first kitchen the new cook has to learn to turn the craft perfected in the classroom into the job. It is in this first workplace where passion has to produce a paycheck. The lessons learned there, the processes, the tools gathered to help make it through the night, resonate louder than the classroom note taking. The habits of the first kitchen are forever imbedded in your culinary vision. Are plates clean and centered, garnished with sprigs of chervil? Or are they busy with *bâtonnets* and *brunoise*?

My first kitchen was at the Prince Michel Vineyard restaurant—a restaurant attached to a well-known winery about forty minutes north of Charlottesville, Virginia. It was spanking clean, enormous, and air-conditioned. The plates were generous fifteen-inch rounds with three-inch pink rims trimmed with gold, and served as a canvas for talented Chef

Alain Lecomte and the visiting chefs from Michelin-starred restaurants in town for special events.

Bright red steamed lobster glistened with drawn butter. We used the tip of a paring knife to balance three beads of caviar around a sprig of chervil for the salmon canapé. The food came together on the plate with order, focus, and precision. Duck breast rested, then was sliced paper thin and fanned alternately with paper-thin slices of peach.

Chef Alain Lecomte taught me that food was beautiful. I watched him as he examined a purveyor's seaweed-covered lobster, swollen-eyed fish with gaping mouths, or scrawny, wrinkled squab. He picked out the diamonds in the rough. Then he'd teach me to painstakingly eviscerate and clean them for him. Chef Lecomte could simmer the flavor and collagen out of a fifty-pound box of veal bones. With yolks, wine, butter, or this bone-fortified water, he would make a sauce to send that fish or squab into the dining room and make believers out of everyone. We could almost hear the dining room erupt in applause when, after the dessert course, Chef wiped the sweat off his face, buttoned the top button of his coat, and pushed open the swinging doors that led out of the kitchen.

For the most part, I was turning vegetables and doing other prep work. I carved carrots, potatoes, and zucchini into eight-sided bullets that not only cooked at the same rate but gave plates a fussed-over look. My first few attempts looked more messed up than fussed over. Even when I thought I'd carved a decent pound or two of potatoes and carrots, Chef would examine the bucketful of my labors. After regarding them very seriously, plunging his hands into the water and letting potatoes and carrots fall through his fingers, he would walk over to the stove and empty the entire contents into a big pot of boiling water. My clumsily carved vegetables disintegrated into what was to become the soup du jour.

After a few weeks I was good enough at turning to be awarded the task of sectioning citrus fruit. Until I got this right, the chef used my knife to make a point of showing me how to separate the peel from the flesh of an orange. If his orange came out perfectly round and skinless and mine did not, it wasn't because of faulty equipment. Chef, who was French, would mumble "Tziz naht ze knife," as he held the blade close, examining it from tip to riveted handle.

When service began I was usually a nervous wreck. I tended the convection oven and responded with a start when the timer rang. One busy Saturday night I had no idea that the towel I used to grab the baked-to-order lime soufflé from the convection oven was damp. "Guilliaahhnn," Chef was shouting, "the soufflé, put it here, hurry, hurry." Steam was bubbling through the towel. But I carried the soufflé to the tray slowly and put it down carefully so that the lightly browned top stayed high above the rim and didn't collapse. The server smiled and raced through the swinging doors. When Sian saw the blisters bubbling through the skin on my fingers and palm, she brushed them with her much smaller hand. "Mommy," she pronounced, awestruck by the sacks of water in my fingers, "what did you do?" I felt kind of silly telling her and her sister that I was carrying a hot soufflé across the kitchen even though the hot dish was blasting steam through the towel and it was burning me. "Why didn't you just put it down?" Magalee asked. I told her that I just couldn't. "There are some things you just can't put down, or drop," I told her, trying to explain. "People are counting on you."

It was an invigorating and invaluable time, but after nearly six months I realized it was also time to move on. I needed to work closer to home. My commute was nearly eighty miles each way. At night on the way home I'd set my cruise control on ninety miles per hour just to catch a glimpse of my two daughters before they fell asleep. I also needed to support both of them—not to mention myself—and graduate from making five dollars an hour as a vegetable cook. The little vineyard restaurant was an opportunity for me to learn, and it helped me realize that cooking in a restaurant was what I really wanted to do. But, as a single mom and sole supporter of our family, I needed to move quickly up the ranks. I didn't have the luxury of learning on the job for years before moving up.

In all my time at the vineyard restaurant, I was never allowed to be at the stove during service. My heart swelled as I watched Chef making art, but standing close and handing him plates was no longer enough. Watching him work was exhilarating and frustrating. I'd never know if I could do this—if I could make food do what he made it do—if I never burned my hands on a ladle or got my chef coat dirty. I had to find a line-cook job to see if I had the talent or skill to do what I wanted more than any big marketing contract or advertising campaign. I knew that if I hoped to one day become a chef myself, I would have to earn that right with hard work and exhausting nights on the line. If I couldn't hack it, I would have to find something else, maybe even give up on my dream.

Having worked in the corporate world for years, I was certain that to get to the top I'd have to get into a high-profile restaurant where the chef's reputation would help open doors for me down the road. But I couldn't just toil under a famous chef. I needed a job that would allow me to support my family. I not only wanted to move to a high-profile restaurant, I wanted to skip a step in the process. Most restaurants want a cook to have done at least a year at the *garde-manger* or salad station before becoming a line cook, but with a move to the more prestigious hot side of the line, I could get both a career and a pay boost all in one shot. ·

So with eleven years in marketing communications under my belt, I crafted a resume that convinced Chef Susan Lindeborg of the popular Morrison-Clark Inn to put me on the grill station. Lucky for me, she was shorthanded at the time. It was a real break, but it was time for me to put up or shut up.

Susan Lindeborg was making beautiful food at the Morrison-Clark Inn. It was all over town. There were great reviews and magazine articles. Her knowledge about the raw ingredients all of us work with was unparalleled. But she had a passionate respect for the spring pea as well as for the lobe of foie gras. When a cook working the line with me made the polenta with so much butter and cream that the corn pudding tasted like scrambled eggs, Susan turned red-faced and didn't quit lecturing until a fresh pot of water had started to boil. Spring peas arrived one day, and, boy, was that sauté cook in trouble when he presented her the special to look over and the peas had been blanched and blended into a glossy pastel purée. "What did you do to the peas?" she shrieked.

Her devotion to food was matched only by her devotion to her staff, from the pastry chef to the dishwasher. A towering figure—she stands about five feet eleven inches tall—she was concerned with all of our lives and careers. I don't think I realized how tough she was until I saw her cleaning the lid that covered the reach-in cooler at the *garde-manger* station. I had looked away from the catfish I was browning when I heard metal clatter against metal. Blood was spurting from the gash along the length of her thumb. Without a word Susan headed for her office. She came back and pitched in plating salads and desserts when we became busy. Her thumb was wrapped tightly in the masking tape she kept in the first aid kit.

Every member of the staff feared, respected, and loved Susan. Sure she'd shout our ears off when we did something wrong. But if she came by when I was reducing the rabbit stock with a little bit of bourbon and broke the glossy surface with her index finger to taste it as I incorporated the butter and it met her expectations, I earned her signature pat on the shoulder. We all strived for that.

Sweat poured from my brow the first minute of the first day I settled into the hot corner of that kitchen. Gas jets on the grill heated lava rocks to about 400 degrees, cooking almost everything I'd learned in cooking school right out of my brain. The sheer intensity of the heat in combination with my jittery nerves made for unforgivable errors. I was an incompetent marker; instead of the neat black squares decorating my T-bone, there were multiple brown and black diagonal stripes. I was slow and disorganized.

My home-cook instincts were in the way. Anyone could tell that I hadn't spent very much time in front of a professional stove. Everything near the stove was branding-iron hot. I reached for pot handles without thinking to pad my hand with one of the thick white towels rationed out to us at the beginning of the shift. The heat blasting from the oven made me hesitate before pulling out the lamb I was finishing to medium well. I jumped back from the heat like an amateur. Tables waited as I fumbled with tongs. I over-reduced sauces and had to start over. I sprinkled too much salt or too little. Susan would check on me now and again and merely sigh. I was sure my first day would be my last.

I had to last, though. As much as this was a challenge, it was too good an opportunity for me to lose. This was a great restaurant. It was located in a historic building in the heart of downtown Washington. Beautiful guest rooms, ornately decorated dining rooms, antique furniture, and the largest floral arrangements I'd ever seen. It was a fine, expensive restaurant, and the food was on the same high level as the décor and the service.

When I finally arrived home after that first day—all burnt and weary, feeling as if I'd fallen asleep on a blanket at the beach—the young girl I'd hired to watch my two children had a laundry list of mishaps to tell me about. Sian hadn't eaten lunch or dinner. Magalee had been caught daydreaming during class and had not turned in a stitch of homework the entire week. Both girls had refused to take a bath, brush their teeth, wear pajamas, or even go to their rooms—let alone to bed. When I followed the babysitter, dragging my exhausted frame into the living room, they were both asleep in front of the TV

wearing last year's Halloween costumes, my jewelry, and lip-
stick Sian had found under the swings during recess.

I couldn't very well say, "Wait till your father gets home."
And I couldn't just go to bed as if nothing had happened. The
babysitter eased the door shut on her way out while I carried
Tinker Bell and Pocahontas, one by one, up to bed. I was too
tired to dress them in their pajamas, but I did wet a washcloth
and wipe the lipstick away.

After they were safely tucked in, I came back downstairs,
put up a pot of coffee, sat down, and read my notes from cooking school. I reread the chapters on grilling, but like Magalee
in class, my eyes couldn't focus on the pages. I read the same
sentence twelve times. My weary mind began to visualize my
worst nightmares: Sian becoming even skinnier than she already was, her ribs in plain view for every judgmental person to
see; Magalee older, the spark gone from her eyes, shopping for
baby formula with food stamps. What would become of my
children while I selfishly chased a dream of cooking for a living? Was it a dream worth chasing? Was it even something that
I could do?

I didn't sleep that night. My shift started at three the following afternoon, so I figured if I stayed up, I'd have time to regroup. The chef wasn't happy with my performance and
neither was I—and I wasn't happy with my performance as a
mother either. I poured myself another cup of coffee and con-
templated what to do. I realized that I needed a specific plan to
excel at both parenting and cooking, and to be able to do both
simultaneously.

First and foremost, I realized that the girls were disobeying,
acting out, and daydreaming because they were seeing less and

less of me. They needed to know that I loved them while familiar things were gone and routines were disrupted. There had been a sudden and unexpected change in their family structure, a move to a new house, and a new school. Something in their lives had to be solid, consistent, and unwavering. That something had to be me.

As for my cooking, I needed to put my first day behind me and actually believe in a significant point I stressed on my resume, the one my new boss had commented on: "It says here that you can cook. We'll have to see about that."

By the time I'd figured things out enough to calm down and study my notes, the sun was coming up. I was physically exhausted but emotionally rejuvenated. I woke the girls, stripped them of their Halloween costumes, and put them in the tub. I told them to get cleaned and dressed in twenty minutes and there'd be corn-flour waffles with strawberry syrup for breakfast.

I usually reserved this for our big Sunday brunch, but brunch was a meal we could no longer share now that I was working as a cook. I found, however, that the unexpected treat could be just as effective as an expected punishment. Not even Sian could resist waffles made with corn flour so that they had a sweet crispness and a golden color.

In fifteen minutes the girls were dressed for school and Magalee was making an awkward attempt at brushing Sian's tangled mess of hair. After breakfast I helped them with their coats and we walked to school.

Our fifteen-minute walk became an every-morning routine and an important part of my parenting. We'd walk the ten blocks in rain, cold, or snow. I learned about their schoolmates, teachers, and the things that worried them. Sian's fears and primary focus tended to be social in nature—she was always seeking company and wanted to be surrounded by people. Magalee craved time to herself and her own thoughts. Sian was a fast-moving bundle of energy, while Magalee sometimes wasn't even aware school had let out for the day. When the babysitter watched them, Magalee had an infinite number of questions for her and was sincerely interested in every answer. Sian had infinite things about herself to tell the babysitter. Magalee never took the position of know-it-all, but Sian—in part because she was three years younger—could be insistent, stubborn, and challenging.

On this first morning we were early. I let the girls loose on the swings and went in to talk to their teachers. The girls went to a school where most of their classmates were from wealthy families. Most of the mothers threw on a fur coat, piled the kids into the Mercedes, and sped off to school. I was well aware of the bad rap that blue-collar working moms got: that they weren't very interested in their kids' education. And at first, it probably seemed that I fit that bill, too. I needed their teachers to know that I would be just as involved as any other mother, if not more, in my daughters' education.

One benefit of restaurant work was that most of my mornings were free, so I volunteered to chaperone field trips and help out at any other activity that had the typical elementary-school teacher crying for help. I cooked Hasty Pudding on a hot plate when Magalee's second-grade class studied Early American history. The story of Johnny Appleseed was distinguished when Magalee showed up for class with fresh apple fritters. I read *Green Eggs and Ham* to Sian and her pre-kindergarten class and brought green deviled eggs and ham, made with avocado and parsley (which I still make today at my restaurant) that Sian sprinkled with grated ham and passed around to her classmates. There was no reason a mother who was also a working cook could not be an asset to the class, and especially to her children.

I went to work that afternoon nervous about my cooking, but feeling a little better about my parenting. There was a meat-loaf in its sauce ready to be reheated, and a note for the babysitter. I gave her the authority to withhold dessert should either of her two charges disobey. As for my second and third days at the grill, I tried to remember the most meaningful things François, my instructor at cooking school, had said during his lectures on technique. His maxim, "Cooking is simply controlling the moisture in food," became my mantra. I practiced making perfect grill marks by placing a lettuce leaf at 11:00 and after a few minutes, rotating it to 2:00. I oiled the grill well and did it again with crusts of bread. By dinnertime my grill marks were perfect. I was ready to tackle that T-bone. I used the same sort of calculated problem-solving for everything I had to do.

I became better as the days went on, but I was far from perfect. I was in big trouble when I overestimated the amount of dried porcini mushrooms I needed. I added two pounds of the expensive ingredient to the risotto special when eight ounces would have been plenty. And, worse, I overcooked the risotto. My mistake cost the restaurant seventy-five dollars. I kept my head up and continued to try to prove myself. But I was getting very anxious, especially after hearing Susan tell the servers, "If anyone has a problem with their lamb or salmon tonight, just let them know we've got a trainee on the grill."

I couldn't argue. Susan just said aloud what I knew to be true. Maybe a younger cook would have been hurt and angry. But at thirty-two, I could accept it and be honest with myself.

Susan gave me a week or two to catch up, but soon, like the rest of the cooks, I needed to come up with a soup of the day. This was our contribution to the menu; it was the chef's way of testing us, but also an honor if she chose yours. I worried. I pored through magazines and cookbooks before settling on a yellow pepper purée. "They'll be paying six-fifty for a bowl of this soup, remember that," Susan reminded me. I combined it with another recipe. I prepared to present my idea to Susan: a yellow pepper soup topped with scallop ceviche and *pico de gallo*. The other cooks warned me that Susan might not go for scallops in springtime. But by that time, it was too late to come up with another plan. I presented my idea and held my breath. I was shocked to hear Susan say, "Okay, order a case of the peppers and a gallon of the twenty–thirty scallops."

My soup was on the menu. My soup. I tried to play it cool and pretended not to be listening when the servers were given their instructions for the evening and Susan told them about the soup of the day—*my* soup of the day. But I wanted to run up into the elegant and quiet dining room in my food-stained apron and clunky work boots and watch the customers order and eat my bright yellow concoction. I had done a chef thing. It was one giant step in the right direction.

• • •

During those first few weeks some of the toughest things I was learning to deal with were the stress of being on my feet for eight hours and the intense heat. When I first started working there, I couldn't bring myself to drink out of a pitcher like the other cooks. When José went up to get us drinks, he handed me my Coke in a half-gallon plastic pitcher like the one that held his lemon water. I demurred and volunteered that I'd be fine with just the ten-ounce plastic cup. "Suit yourself," José said, wiping the sweat from his face with his sleeve and downing about half of his pitcher. But it wasn't long before I was drinking out of a pitcher like the rest of them. It also didn't take long before I stopped fretting over the burns on my arms, and soon lost count of how many I accumulated.

I was one of them, flicking my hot pans noisily into the pile of dirties, tossing tongs onto the handle of the oven door without looking. Hands busy with ladles and whisks, I was closing the oven door with my foot and the door to my fridge with my hips. I was lifting forty-quart pots of browned bones and water, and melting my fingerprints away holding hot plates—not as long as I could stand it, but as long as it took to position the vegetables, spoon the sauce, and center the garnish.

I, too, was answering the phone, "Kitchen!" in a gruff and abrupt tone (to discourage phone calls to the busiest room in the building). I was making the soup once a week as well as the brunch special.

My first days on the grill were so difficult and exhausting, I really started to doubt myself. Now, months later, I could put those awkward days behind me. I was finally comfortable cooking for a living. At the end of each shift I could tell I was getting stronger. All that I'd seen in kitchens at school, at the vineyard, and at my father's stove was coming together. The doubts were evaporating and I started to believe in myself. The grilled T-bone with caramelized onion-jalapeño chutney was the most expensive item on the menu. It sold like crazy every Tuesday—one of the nights I worked the grill. "They know Tuesday is a good night for the T-bone," Susan said, looking at me over her reading glasses while scanning the night's numbers. "Sure," she continued—my expression obviously suggesting she was exaggerating. "The servers know. They wouldn't push it if they thought it would be coming back to the kitchen."

Believing I could do this job was ninety percent of the battle. It gave me the confidence, the backbone to say to myself, "Okay, that's medium. Plate it, spoon the sauce, toss the chives, and let the server take it out." There are plenty of cooks who fuss over medium until it's medium well, and that's because they lack confidence in their abilities.

To be as successful at home, I also had to believe in how I was raising the girls without their father. It angered and frustrated my ex-husband. He called suggesting that with more counseling we could take another shot at being a family. He told me that I had made mistakes, too. I owed it to him to meet him halfway and work it out. It dismayed my friends and family that I didn't seize an opportunity to be a married woman again. Wouldn't the hardship be over? That might have seemed so to an outsider. But there was something flickering inside me. It needed oxygen and freedom to grow. I was betting that the girls and I could survive these lean times. So I didn't pay much attention when my mother referred to me as the "corporate dropout." The girls would have a better role model if they saw me attack the difficulties surrounding us without compromise. If I succeeded on the more difficult path, and they witnessed it, I could set the example I longed to set.

I had to bring the girls on board and make them feel like part of a team. We made a pact to be flexible. There would be disappointments as we struggled through this period in our lives, I warned them. But, as corny as it sounded, we would always try to look on the bright side.

The talk yielded results. I got them to take care of their personal hygiene without being hounded. They began to treat the babysitter with more respect. They agreed to take turns setting the table and letting me know when we were out of milk.

Our lives were different now, and no matter how young they were, we could not hide from it or pretend things hadn't changed. Hiding things never worked. My first lesson in this was when I tried to avoid the "death discussion" by walking quickly past a dead cat in the street near school. Despite my best efforts to protect them from a side of life they didn't yet know or understand, their own curiosity got the best of them.

"Look, Sian, a dead cat!" shouted Magalee, running over to get a closer look with Sian right behind her.

I found that it was better to get less than lovely talks like this out of the way as soon as possible, and that included the one about their absentee father. I could not let them continue to believe that our lives would go on as if nothing had happened.

While I knew that I had to stay the course on my career and on pursuing the life I wanted, this also meant that there would have to be compromises, including some of the rituals we had come to expect. We all had to be okay with that. Sunday brunch was moved to Saturday. I promised that I would find the time to take them out on Halloween, but it would be an early evening as I would have to go to work right afterward.

At the vineyard and as the P.M. grill cook at the Morrison-Clark Inn, I never called in sick or requested a change in the schedule. I wouldn't have been very marketable as a cook if word got around that my single-mother status made me a problematic hire. I knew that people probably assumed that I would need more time off because of my daughters, but I made sure that everyone learned this wasn't the case at all. While younger cooks were switching with me to get the day off for this party or that concert, I was building a reputation as the most reliable member of the staff.

I wanted the girls to see how hard I worked and how committed I was. No matter how tired I might have been at the end of the week, I kept my promises, to them and to my employer. I broke the news to Magalee that I could not find the time to see her play the goose in her class production of *Charlotte's Web*. But I would be able to make it to her viola recital—although I would be coming directly from a daytime shift smelling of food.

My daughters watched as I worked my way through the Morrison-Clark Inn kitchen from grill to sauté. I was now bolder with my recommendations for the soup of the day when my turn at it came around. A hot chicken consommé poured from the waiter's elegant coffee server over a warm bowl of rice, steamed shrimp, and chiffonade of spinach received a raised eyebrow from Chef Lindeborg. "We'll have to see how this one plays out," she said suspiciously. She liked the idea, but questioned the servers' ability to pull it off. Years later, long after I had a kitchen of my own, I visited the Morrison-Clark Inn and I ordered the soup. The waiter placed the warm bowl in front of me. In the bottom were scallions precisely sliced on the bias and croutons, freshly toasted and tossed in butter and herbs. From his coffee server, he poured a cream-spiked tomato purée to the rim of the bowl. This was probably the best pat on the back I ever got from Susan.

The greatest thing about Susan was that nothing got past her. She paid attention. She knew how we worked and what we could handle. She could see which of us had talent and drive. Susan looked out for us. When she knew it was time for me to move on she steered me in the direction of Ann Cashion. I had heard from other cooks that Ann, a future James Beard Award winner, was about to open a place in town and that her concept was revolutionary. Cashion's Eat Place used only the freshest products in season, mostly from small local farmers— locally raised lamb, goat cheese from a guy who drove his truck down from Pennsylvania's Amish country. The menu would feature a few core items but otherwise it would change daily.

Ann was looking for the best and the brightest. She was working to put together an ambitious and smart line crew that could handle the changing ingredients and menu. Ann had cooked for Alice Waters at Chez Panisse and had cranked pasta in Tuscany. Harvard educated and tireless, she knew food and what it could and couldn't do. Flavors and textures were there to make the plate of food a portrait of balance and harmony. Unlike Susan's kitchen, there was no book of recipes. Ann insisted we use our instincts and let color, taste, and texture bring us to the final product. After a week of pre-opening training we were nervous but ready. Ann always seemed to know what to say and that night when the doors opened and the seats began to fill, she told us to be proud. There was a collective chest swelling among us and we knew that we were on the brink of something great. We were the ones bringing great food to the city. The world was depending upon us. How could we fail?

For me it was a life-changing experience. The success of the restaurant depended upon all of us learning to cook in what became known as "The Cashion's Fashion." And this was my first restaurant opening—lessons learned here would surely pay off in the future. This opening crew at Cashion's had to learn to make the menu work; there was no one to teach us how to set up and organize the sauté or grill for the night. Ann showed us the way she wanted the mashed potatoes done and how the chicken should be roasted. But it was up to us to come up with the tricks that made the night go smoothly. There was no experienced old line cook working the station for years whom we could rely on to show us how to work faster and more efficiently to stay ahead of the orders. We were the "old line cooks."

There was a lot of fumbling around during those first weeks. The corn puddings could not be unmolded without breaking; the polenta in the grilled stuffed squid swelled beyond its boundaries. We had plenty of time to fix things when the hot DC summer slowed business down. We could see worry overtake Ann's unwavering certainty and confidence. She cut back on our hours. (I had to take a second job.)

Then the review we'd all been waiting for came out. It wasn't long before we shot well past the goal of 100 covers for the night. From then on it was a race from the minute I came in for me to have my station ready by 5:30. Still, I found time to take a minute and sharpen my knife. I was showing a new cook how to bring back an edge when I found Ann's too dull to cut butter. I jokingly chided her before taking hers to the stone.

In my two years with Ann, I was promoted from sauté cook to *sous*-chef. I trained staff, perfected recipes, headed the brunch operation, and added a few items to the daily-changing menu—there was the stewed veal tossed with Ann's house-made capellini, the corn relish with the crab cakes, and the whitefish quenelles. The Alsatian onion tart that I made one evening received media attention. I had become not just one of those sought-after line cooks, but a leader. Ann noticed. And when a couple of young, anxious-looking attorneys-turned-restaurateurs visited the restaurant and asked her to suggest a chef to run the kitchen in the new place they were planning to open in a tiny but growing DC suburb, she told them about me.

CORN-FLOUR WAFFLES
WITH STRAWBERRY SYRUP

It's the corn flour that makes these waffles so unique.
Masa harina, as it's called at the local Latin market where
I can always find it, makes the waffles crisp and light.

MAKES 20 WAFFLES

2 CUPS FLOUR

1 3/4 CUPS CORN FLOUR (MASA HARINA)

2 TABLESPOONS SUGAR

5 TEASPOONS BAKING POWDER

2 TEASPOONS SALT

3 EGGS

1/2 CUP BUTTERMILK

3 CUPS WHOLE MILK

1/4 CUP VEGETABLE OIL

THE SYRUP

1 PINT STRAWBERRIES

1/2 CUP SUGAR

1/4 CUP WATER

Sift together all the dry ingredients into a large bowl. In a
separate bowl beat the eggs and then whisk in the buttermilk
and milk. Pour the well-blended liquid ingredients into the
dry ingredients. Mix gently but thoroughly. Let stand at
room temperature for 5 minutes, then whisk in the oil.

Heat a waffle iron and brush it well with oil. While the iron is getting hot, wash, trim, and slice in half the strawberries. Place the berries in a heavy stainless-steel saucepan with the sugar and water. Simmer over low heat until the liquid is reduced and the berries are quite soft. Strain and set aside.

Cook the waffles on the iron according to specifications and directions for your equipment. If you don't have a waffle iron, pancakes are a great substitution: Follow all of the above steps, except use a heavy-bottomed skillet and heat 2 tablespoons of oil over medium heat. Spoon 1/4 cup of the batter into the skillet. When bubbles form on the top and the edges of the cake start to brown, turn the pancake with a spatula. Cook on the other side for another 2 or 3 minutes, or until steam begins to rise from the pancake. Remove from the skillet.

Keep the cooked waffles (or pancakes) warm in a 200-degree oven. Serve with cold butter and the strawberry syrup.

HASTY PUDDING

I taught English my first year out of college and was fascinated that an epic poem inspired by this simple recipe of boiled cornmeal could have survived two hundred years and is still studied in American classrooms today. It is the quintessential comfort food and distinctly American.

MAKES 6 SIDE-DISH SERVINGS

2 CUPS WATER

1/2 CUP STONE-GROUND CORNMEAL

I TEASPOON SALT

3 TABLESPOONS BUTTER

Bring the water to a boil. Whisk in the cornmeal and salt. Lower the heat and simmer, stirring constantly with a wooden spoon. Allow the mixture to simmer for about 30 minutes. Stir in the butter and serve.

APPLE FRITTERS

These make an appearance on my menu every now and again. Nothing is more simply satisfying. Tart apples balance the rich, crisply fried coating. I've caught some folks in the dining room abandoning the knife and fork when eating these.

MAKES ABOUT 25 FRITTERS

VEGETABLE OIL FOR FRYING

6 BRAEBURN OR MCINTOSH APPLES, PEELED, CORED, AND SLICED INTO RINGS

JUICE OF I LEMON

2 CUPS FLOUR

I TABLESPOON BAKING POWDER

I TABLESPOON SUGAR

1/4 TEASPOON SALT

2 EGGS

3/4 CUP MILK

1/4 CUP APPLE JUICE

Heat the vegetable oil in a deep fryer to 350 degrees. Or, if you are using oil in a pan on the stove, you will need about 2 inches of oil in a deep pan. Heat this carefully over medium heat.

Toss the apple rings with the lemon juice and set aside. Sift the dry ingredients together into a large bowl. In a separate bowl, beat the eggs and blend in the milk and juice. Stir the wet ingredients into the dry. Combine completely but gently. Dip the apple rings into the batter and allow excess to drip off. Place the rings into the oil a few at a time and fry for 3 minutes per side. If you're using a deep fryer, lower the basket. Drop three or four batter-coated rings into the hot oil and cook for 3 minutes.

Drain on paper towels or brown paper bags.

GREEN DEVILED EGGS AND HAM

The Dr. Seuss–inspired whimsical approach to deviled eggs took a little bit of thought. Adding flavor and color to bright yellow yolks without adding any artificial coloring, and in a combination that kids would eat, was one of the biggest challenges of my career.

MAKES 24 DEVILED EGGS

12 EGGS

1/2 CUP HEAVY CREAM

1 AVOCADO, PEELED AND SEEDED

1/3 CUP FLAT-LEAF PARSLEY LEAVES

1 TEASPOON SALT

1/4 TEASPOON CAYENNE PEPPER

1/4 CUP MINCED HAM

Place the 12 eggs in a pot large enough for all of them to rest on the bottom. Cover the eggs with cold water, so that there are 4 inches of water above the top surface of the eggs. Bring the water to a boil, cover the pot, and turn off the heat. Let the eggs sit in the hot water, covered, for 11 minutes. Drain and place the eggs in an ice-water bath. After 5 minutes, re-move them from their shells. Set to dry on a towel.

Carefully cut the eggs in half and remove the yolks. Cut a small, flat spot on each half of the boiled egg-white cups so that they lay flat on a platter. Set aside in the refrigerator. Place the yolks in a bowl and break them into a powder with a whisk. In a blender on the lowest setting blend half the cream with the avocado, parsley, salt, and pepper. Do this gently and carefully; you do not want to make whipped cream here. Pour this mixture from the blender into the bro-ken yolks. Whisk the green cream and yolks to make a smooth whipped cream. Fill a star-tipped pastry bag with the mixture and pipe a good tablespoon or so into the halved egg whites. If you don't have a pastry bag, you can fill the eggs by spooning about a tablespoon of the filling into each half. Garnish with the minced ham.

STEAMED SHRIMP AND SPINACH
IN CONSOMMÉ

It was a simple broth that I had at a Japanese restaurant that inspired this soup. Eating out often gets my wheels turning.

MAKES 4 SOUP-COURSE SERVINGS

3 QUARTS LOW-SODIUM CHICKEN STOCK

12 MEDIUM SHRIMP (ABOUT ½ POUND), PEELED, DEVEINED, AND SLICED IN HALF LENGTHWISE

1 CUP COOKED WHITE RICE, JASMINE OR BASMATI

1 CUP FRESH SPINACH, SLICED THINLY

1 TEASPOON SALT

¼ TEASPOON FRESHLY GROUND WHITE PEPPER

In a large soup pot, boil the stock until it is reduced by half. Turn off the heat and add the shrimp to the pot. Let the shrimp sit in the hot stock until they turn pink and curl into loose springs, about 5 minutes. Remove them from the stock and arrange six springs of shrimp in each bowl. Center ¼ cup of rice that has been pressed into a buttered shot glass and unmolded. Sprinkle the spinach over the rice and the shrimp. Season the stock with the salt and pepper. Strain the hot stock into a pitcher or soup terrine and ladle some of the hot stock into each bowl.

Two

THE FOOD IS MORE IMPORTANT THAN YOUR FEELINGS

There is a certain security in cooking for a talented chef. A cook just does exactly as he's told and the food turns out just as everyone expected. But a good cook needs to make adjustments and ask questions—can it be done faster, can it be better, can it be consistently perfect night after night? Then there are the times when a chef has an idea, a thought—not quite worked out, but a vision. It is the great cook, the talented cook, who can take that vision and make it work.

Maybe it's a red-wine reduction done *"à la minute"* with garlic over a seared tenderloin. It's never been done in the kitchen, just talked about. We open in five minutes. Get some red wine and garlic for your station and make it happen. This is when that good cook sweats—not from the heat coming from that eight-burner range, but from the challenge of going from good to great.

It takes time to go from the awkward beginner to the competent professional with brain and body working together. All that information about heat, moisture, flour, butter, salt, and collagen becomes integrated with instinct. When you have accomplished this, producing great food in a high-pressure setting appears effortless. Accepting and overcoming the challenges along the way kicks all that into gear. It was the red-wine reduction that got me noticed. Regulars started by writing me notes or sending the server to my little sauté corner of the kitchen with a glass of Châteauneuf-du-Pape from the bottle at their table.

There was nothing quite like having my work appreciated by customers. Sure it's the chef's food, but for the first time in my career, my talent as a cook was being recognized. When my onion tart appeared on the menu, it was mentioned in the annual dining guide written by the local critic. The critics were giving food that I had created their stamp of approval. There was potentially a receptive audience for what I could produce in a kitchen. I could succeed under the right circumstances. Maybe it would be in a little out-of-the-way spot in the suburbs, not necessarily an award winner, but I would be satisfied being famous, loved, and appreciated by my regular customers. All I needed now was the right opportunity.

It unexpectedly happened a few months before my thirty-fifth birthday. I was aflutter with nerves. It didn't seem too long ago that I was hacking away at carrots in the vineyard kitchen. Now I was about to be leading my own kitchen. I met the owners of Evening Star Café at the site—a corner bar in a transitioning Northern Virginia neighborhood. They were a newly married lawyer couple with big ideas and a little bit of cash. They lived a few blocks away and had mentioned to the local realtor that they'd like to be part of the fledgling business corridor. When the Snuggery Café went on the market, they pounced. All they needed now was a chef.

Ann had talked me up pretty good to them. But the proof was in the crab cakes. I won them over with a recipe I had been working on for years. My well-practiced roasted chicken sealed the deal. This was the easy part; now I had to make my recipes work for ninety-five seats at tables, thirty at the bar, and twenty on the patio, weather permitting. I accepted the job without hesitation, but my heart was pounding.

I had to really work at visualizing myself in charge of this kitchen in what was once a dive bar and a neighborhood sore spot. But over the months the contractors transformed the space into a bright yellow-and-red dining room and bar. Meanwhile, I designed an adequate working space in the tiny kitchen, and spent hours calming my nerves designing the menu and developing a plan for how the grill, sauté, and salad stations would put out food for ninety-five diners.

During my many years sorting through recipes in magazines and reading cookbooks, I had developed a considerable food filing cabinet in my brain. There were inklings and notions and images. I had read somewhere that cabbage goes great with salmon. I took a bone out of a chicken leg the same way I had seen Craig Claiborne do it on television. I piped it full of a crayfish mousse and poached it the way Craig had demonstrated. I had seen a picture of caramelized pearl onions and thought that they would look great cascading over a thick round cut of beef tenderloin. I had experimented with crabmeat and veal. And I had come pretty close to roasting the perfect chicken.

Now it was time to put all of those thoughts about food on

paper and make them come alive. I thought about food constantly. I read over my collection of clipped recipes and thought about all of the elements that go into a well-balanced plate. I listened when the words of wisdom came back to me— they were all in my head, reminding me about texture and color. Pascal, François, Alain, Susan, and Ann were in there wagging a finger or nodding approvingly. I started out with a blank piece of paper. In about a month, with input from the owners (there had to be a few representatives from Cajun cuisine and nothing could be over twenty dollars), I had my menu. I shuddered to think that I would have to do this again. When the seasons changed or a selection on the menu just wasn't selling or needed to be retired, I would have to subject myself again to this mind wringing. Coming up with this summary in food of everything the restaurant represents—the dreams and ambitions of the chef and owners—is as exhilarating, exhausting, exciting, and terrifying as having a baby.

Still, the menu is a list of directions—it's not even a road map. There's still a lot of work to be done before anyone gets from point A (an empty cooler and not even an onion diced) to point B (a dining room full of people, each of them eating and loving what's on the plate in front of them). With the menu out of the way for now, I could focus on point A.

I scrubbed old grease off the walls and mopped the floor over and over again. There were hot, endless afternoons testing equipment and recipes. I spent long mornings waiting for the health department.

Sleep was interrupted when anxiety seeped into my dreams. One fitful night the produce came in splintered wooden crates. Later in that dream, the green onions had me

in a cold sweat—they just weren't right—when on closer ex-
amination I realized that it was really a fifty-pound crate of
huge white onions spray-painted the color of a traffic light.

The hand-wringing days and cold sweats at night were
those new-chef nerves. I was dealing with the low budget of a
new restaurant put together with low-interest loans and the
limited cash of the young owners. Plus I was a young, untested
chef—I didn't attract the cooks on their way up the ladder the
way my former bosses did. My staff consisted of a couple of
older has-beens, a dishwasher-turned-cook who was living in a
shelter after running away from her abusive husband, a recovering alcoholic, and a terribly farsighted diabetic who had
been burning pork chops and grilled cheese in this very
kitchen when it was a dive.

I was petrified that they'd never get it. The restaurant
would be a dismal failure or, worse, poison someone. To mask
my fear I figured I needed to develop a chef persona. I started
with the mean chef. I threw tantrums and yelled whenever the
veal chop wasn't done right or no one had cleaned the squid in
time for service. The hard-boiled crew was unfazed—they'd
been yelled at, shot at, smacked around, who knows what else.
Moreover, none of them understood the importance of being
on time, or could tell when the succotash had turned, or knew
the proper way to roast a pork loin.

These were people from a side of the tracks I had never
walked. I'd never even seen a book of food stamps until my
salad cook took the booklet out of her bra and handed her
nine-year-old son a sweaty, crumpled coupon and told him to
get something to eat before spending the rest of the evening
home alone. This was definitely not the kitchen staff of over-

achievers I had worked alongside at Cashion's. There was no great ambition in the group I gathered in the kitchen for training week. This was a group just doing what it took to get by. I was a snob—shaking my head and not sure how to talk to these people. We had nothing in common.

This was never more apparent than on that first Friday payday. I was prepping by myself in this kitchen low on financial resources and I was running out of time. The big hand on the clock was whizzing around so fast it was taking my breath away. I was panting and soaking my shirt and apron with perspiration from washing the pots and pans I needed. There was no way I was going to get the soup made, sauces reduced, and vegetables blanched. Here I was with the menu's entire *mise en place* (in English—things in place: all of the components and garnishes to complete the menu items) on my shoulders. I was feeling desperate and utterly alone. Just when I was ready to give up and sink to the floor in chest-heaving sobs, the door to the kitchen swung open. It was Richard. "Hey there, Chef," he said, walking past me to the back of the restaurant. Was it 5:30 already? Last I looked it was just a little before 3:00. Roshena was right behind him. "Hi, Chef," she said, almost singing. Boy, was she in a good mood. Then Ronald—he wasn't even on the schedule for the day. The kitchen heat fogged his Coke-bottle glasses and he nodded at the stand mixer. " 'Scuse me, Chef."

Boy was I wrong about this crew, I was thinking. They all came in early to help me. They must have known I was swamped. I washed my hands and grabbed some clean towels to lay out for them. But Richard breezed by me, still in his street clothes. "See you at five-thirty, Chef." Then came Roshena right behind him. She was wiping her neck with a paper towel and drinking a soda. "I'll be a little late today, Chef," she whispered, "that okay?" Ronald bumped into her on his way back out. "Watch out," he snarled at her. "What is it Chef say, 'No parking on the dance floor.'" He laughed a wicked laugh and they walked out together. Each of them had an envelope, with ragged flaps from being hastily torn open. Their paychecks, they just came to get their paychecks. I sucked back the tears and got to work.

This scene played out on a few more Fridays until Samuel and Roshena didn't show up to work later that day. They had cashed their checks at the liquor store down the street and drank what was left after paying the rent. Payday was moved to Monday. And I convinced the owners to let me hire a prep cook, got better organized, became a better delegator, insisted evening shifts start at 4:00 P.M., and my Fridays got a lot better. Still, our different priorities made the characters of my kitchen tough to manage. There were plenty of low-level power struggles that I was slow to recognize. I was often too nice and lent someone five or ten dollars, never to see it again. Then came the afternoon when I had had enough. My landlord had yelled in my ear that morning and my car was dying. So when Marcus—with his hand out—stopped me on my way to pick up the girls from school, take them home, wait for the sitter, then rush back to work, I exploded. He didn't come back that night so I was stuck washing dishes, dicing carrots, and shaping crab cakes in between loads. The kitchen was uncomfortably quiet that night. But I think we were all crossing a threshold. I guess I thought we had to get along, and that they had to like me. Until the day I lost my temper, my crew had never thought of me as anything but that rich, white-talking black woman they worked for. It took me getting angry for them to see that I had many of the concerns they had about money, landlord, job security—for them to see me as human. I, too, was worried about my kids and the price of milk. How could I be a snob when, like many of them, I had holes in my socks and thread-bare chef pants and work boots that were taking in water? It wasn't important for us to become friends or for the crew to be as devoted to me as I was to my chefs. But we had to have enough trust between us to work together under conditions that some have compared to the trenches of battle.

I lost staff regularly through a revolving door spinning with crack cocaine and misdemeanors. It all became easier when I stopped caring. A few Fridays like the payday where I sweated it out but survived made me realize that no one was indispensable.

It was a Saturday night in early fall when I had my strongest cook, Best, on sauté, and untried Samuel on the grill. I gave this older but soft guy a chance; he was the only cook who kept up with the area food scene and he looked the part. He came to training in checked pants, a new chef coat, and a neckerchief. "I have always wanted to go to Cash Haawwns," he said. I didn't have the heart to tell him Chef Cashion is from Mississippi, not Burgundy. That Saturday we got busy early, and while washing dishes I called out the orders to them. "Best, I need five crab cakes, one tenderloin medium, two medium well." I didn't look up, just snapped the tickets off the printer and ordered appetizers and entrées to be cooked and plated. "Samuel, drop three salmon and two shrimp." Samuel's salmon and shrimp cooked quickly, so I held his tickets for a couple of beats so that food for the table of six would be prepared at roughly the same time.

Best's finished plates were clattering under the heat lamp. Nothing was coming from Sam. "Samuel, give me those salmon. And drop four more." His head was down, but he shouted the appropriate response: "Salmon working, Chef." I looked at his grill. It was clean. He hadn't started cooking anything. I started to rush back to the line and help him when I smelled bourbon—as strong as if he had bathed in it. I grabbed him by the loose cloth of his chef coat and tossed him aside.

Samuel quit the next morning. He claimed to be in the hospital. The women I could hear giggling in the background were his nurses. I could hear that bourbony slur in his voice while he explained his condition to me. Roshena ran into him at the market where many of my staff and folks in the neighborhood traded food stamps for cash to buy cigarettes and cheap liquor. "Chef can't disrespect me like that," he told her. Still, I surprised them all when I fired Best. He had been late to work too many times and had blown off the mandatory staff meeting.

To some measure I earned their respect. Roshena told me I was a "good boss." And when my estranged husband was in town for custody mediation she offered to get someone to beat him up for me. "I'll tell him you're my boss and he'll do it for a free meal . . . or for nothin'." I appreciated that they waited until after their shifts to smoke marijuana in the parking lot. I pretended not to know.

But even after coming to terms with the staff issues, there was still trouble. The electricity was cut off right before lunch, then again the next week as we started dinner on Tuesday. The manager emptied the register and rushed over to the power company to pay the delinquent bill. My Friday fish delivery wasn't coming unless I met the driver with a check for all of the fish we'd received since opening day—about three thousand dollars' worth. I felt as if I were losing. The dining room was consistently full at 5:30, and my knife was dull and constantly in motion from 9:00 in the morning till then. There was little time to fix it. And now we were all stumbling through service, producing imperfect food to an increasing number of diners in an unstable environment.

At a mandatory staff meeting I tried to reach beyond the language barriers and the learning disabilities. I struggled to find the words to make them care. I tried to convey the feeling that Ann had stoked in all of us when we'd fired up the ten-burner stove at Cashion's and she'd told us to "be proud."

Here I was trying to wrestle with the brains of a team of cooks and get them to produce my food just as I did, just as I had shown them. But none of these people had my training or experience, and my lone brain wasn't cutting it. We had to sit down and come up with a new brain. Sure, I would be controlling this new brain. But it had to be a collective. It had to come from our shared histories, so that when this brain wanted a roasted chicken, it didn't matter who was cooking, the chicken would be the same.

I appealed to the one link that bound us together—white, black, Latino, alcoholic, abuser, abused, uneducated, and educated. We all had one thing in common: We all chose to make our living in the kitchen. From there we could develop a brain, an identity, our code, a culture of our kitchen—a set of "family values." I had been trying to impose the kitchen culture of other restaurants—the "family values" of other restaurants—onto this team. It was like trying to teach the crew in charge of pulling off Halloween to apply their skills in reproducing Christmas.

This kitchen needed to define itself. Sometimes, as with children, you just have to watch them in action and get to know who they are and what makes them tick. You must allow them to exhibit the behaviors that they enjoy and that inspire them. I realized my tempter-tantrum chef was an empty carica-ture, that in shutting out the personalities I squelched the cre-ativity. I had to realize that my creativity might be the center of the culture and the brain, but others had to be allowed to participate, to chime in. This is where confidence comes from.

I knew this from parenting my children. I let the girls, at ages six and two, participate. They chose the color of their book bags and the variety of cactus for their bedroom. I also al-lowed them to have a say when shopping for clothes and shoes—within reason. This measure of control over some of the smallest things builds confidence.

With our family down by one, the girls and I had to re-create our "family values." Sure it would be similar to the sys-tem in which I was raised, but we were a family of three. We did things differently. The most important part of the process was involving the girls—taking into account what they had to say and who they were when defining us as a family.

It wasn't much different in the kitchen. I ordered the plas-tic bags that Richard insisted would keep the roasted chickens hot and moist until they were ready to be plated. I allowed the kitchen radio to be on all day but, per our kitchen family values, we had to agree on a station. Sure when the Latinos found themselves alone, or when there was a black majority, someone invariably changed the station, but when I walked in, it was quickly switched back to oldies.

I had to admit that this brain had its limitations. Parts of the brain had never gone beyond the eighth grade, and some of those parts had been compromised by drug use. So, I simplified the menu. I replaced the pork loin with a pork chop. We started using cleaned frozen squid rather than fresh. I quit trying to re-create the fine French food of the vineyard. Instead, I focused on the accessible—food my staff could understand. There was a scallion johnnycake with the salmon. Swiss chard wilted with bacon accompanied the rockfish. Still keeping it simple, I introduced seasonal changes that pushed the edges of our kitchen culture. The blueberry gravy with the pork chop showed our playful side. I pushed us higher, too, with a wild mushroom and pearl onion ragout on the tenderloin.

Moreover, I let my guard down. I encouraged them to be open to learning by leading this part of our culture. I let Beth show me that a drop of soap in the water washed the collard greens better. I think it was Cynthia who showed me that water disappearing off of a fast-drying boiled egg meant it was done. When there was a surplus of chicken breast, we poached it. While it cooled, I told Roshena to stop bragging about her chicken salad and make it for an appetizer special. We served it on a leaf of hydroponic Boston lettuce, with a *brunoise* of carrot garnish and brioche toast points cut long and thin—about the size of a ruler—for drama.

I borrowed a page from my parents' book when defining my family at home. Growing up, we were never to use the words "shut up" or to call a sibling "stupid." My mother found these words inflammatory and provocative. With five kids in the house—all pretty close in age—a parent had to be creative to keep fights from breaking out. I didn't let my two little ones use those words either. It also became a rule in my kitchen. And surprisingly, it was adhered to with more discipline than simply coming in to work on time. No cook, dishwasher, or busboy ever insisted someone "shut up" or declared that a coworker was "stupid." There were disagreements in the small, hot space, but nothing escalated to the knife-jabbing brawls I'd heard about.

I couldn't have known, but before my "kitchen culture" meeting, the reviewer had visited our stumbling kitchen. The photographer called and said he was on his way. The magazine needed pictures for the already completed review. He dropped hints as he set up silvery balloons and umbrellas. He was smiling when he said, "Think positive." But his light talk and the happy way he pranced around the dining room bringing light fixtures and glasses of beer into focus didn't stop the churning in my stomach.

When I finally got my hands on a copy, I was in the basement of the empty restaurant, early on a Sunday morning. I felt blindsided. It was the same feeling—being on the receiving end of an unexpected slap—that crept over me at a parent-teacher conference when Magalee's teacher told me that she was going to be held back to repeat the third grade.

As I pulled on my boots, I tried really hard not to look at the pages where words and phrases like "slow," "way too sour," and "does not improve mistakes" bloomed up and out above the black and white. The phone rang. Some guy wanted to know if the étouffée was served during Sunday brunch. I found the word étouffée in the article. It was "smooth and well-seasoned." It was good, the review declared. The phone rang again. This time a woman wanted to know when we opened. Before I could make it upstairs to the kitchen, I had answered the phone ten more times. It was almost 9:00. I unlocked the door for the dishwasher. That morning we did almost 100 people for brunch.

Had that dining room full of people not read what I had read, and what the restaurant owners were crying about? Did they not believe they would be subject to dry and overcooked mussels, a too-sour Vidalia onion confit? I shared the review with my old boss. "It's not bad," I remember Susan saying. "Honestly, look at this. It's telling you all the things you need to do to get better."

My staff never saw the review. They just weren't interested. As long as they could cash their checks and eat their fill during family meal, all was right with the world. Like the gathering around my table at home where my father spooned rice beside our pork chop and then ladled the gravy over it all, the "family" table at a restaurant is also a safe place to let it out and be yourself. We got to know each other around the table or sitting on milk crates in the kitchen, our plates on our knees. The meal taken together—after one of the cooks blended leftovers in his or her own unique way—broke the stress of the day.

I skipped family meal the week the review came out. I was in a potentially contagious funk and questioning my ability as a chef. And with Magalee about to fail the third grade I was feeling as if I were failing on all fronts. Maybe Susan had been right. When I told her about landing this job she was support-ive but skeptical. She was hoping that I'd work under a number of chefs and get as much valuable experience as possible. I'd been clipping good and bad reviews and recipes, collecting menus, and voraciously reading all of the old cookbooks she'd picked up for me while she shopped for antique linens out in the country. But I needed this boost, this career change, to pay the rent and to feed my children.

I took Susan's advice and wrote the reviewer a letter. I thanked her for taking the time to consider writing about my small, young kitchen. It was cathartic and helped me get past it and move on. I looked at the criticism for what it was. The reviewer was right. The onion confit didn't work. It had to go. There was no one on my staff besides me who knew how to steam mussels until they were just done—I took them off the menu. I disagreed about the pecan-crusted rockfish. The roasted garlic sauce with it made perfect sense. And as for the pork chop with caramelized brandy sauce—it was a top seller. It had to stay, too.

And since our kitchen now had a culture, a group identity, the collective brain could be retrained. The things we couldn't master left the menu. Other menu items were exhaustively re-examined and worked over. We got better. And the following reviews praised the roasted chicken and called the mashed po-tatoes "the best anywhere." One magazine listed us as one of the twenty new restaurants to watch.

Another photographer called. This time they wanted pic-tures of me, not just of my food. I was to be one of three chefs included in a piece on up-and-coming culinary talent. I was under the radar, and the local media was taking notice. The exposure brought more people to the restaurant. I was developing a following. There were now people who were fans of my food. It was the beginning.

The slap spurred me into action with my daughter in that case as well. We took a week of vacation in the spring and with workbooks and Scholastic computer games, I taught Magalee everything she missed in the three years she'd been drifting off into space and spending class time gazing out the window. She took the standardized test with her class and the 145 questions, missed only seven. Ms. Raiche had no choice but to recommend Magalee's advancement to fourth grade.

Reviews that followed were better. And there was more media coverage—even a spot on public access cable. The positive feedback was great for morale—mine, especially. It was enough of a bump to my ego to give me the confidence to fill my boots a little better and lead the kitchen. The crew responded by producing high-quality food like a well-oiled machine. And Magalee was with her friends and peers in the fourth grade. What had I done?

With the great reviews and word of mouth, people were coming from all over to eat at the little place where a young chef was bringing "a quiet sophistication to simple food." But the stress of serving hundreds more customers a week was trying the new brain. There were longer hours and work intensified. Tempers flared. There were times when I walked in on shouting matches and cooks on the verge of coming to blows in the tiny open kitchen that was hot and cramped.

Magalee was in the fourth grade and struggling. She certainly had the ability to do fourth-grade work; however, she had never developed proper study and homework habits. Until she did, she would have years of bad report cards and parent-teacher meetings ahead of her in which no one was smiling.

I was learning that like my family, my kitchen staff, no matter how much emotional energy I put into each individual, would never let me rest either. Many of these adults had problems that made their work in the kitchen insignificant. No one valued the place as I did. That's natural. I was the chef. It was my name in the papers. I had everything at stake. It was a difficult acknowledgment—I couldn't make them care as I did. One cook was being evicted; another had a son arrested for sexual assault. Bonnie, my prep cook, was fired by the manager before I arrived at work one morning. She was caught sneaking drinks from the bar inventory—an offense that called for immediate termination in the employee manual. I recruited new staff and integrated them into the kitchen culture. Things would be going great, and then tragedy would strike and we'd lose another to the court system or to the bottle.

Running a functional kitchen was more like parenting than I'd ever imagined. I found myself encouraging a cook to continue drug counseling, translating a parole violation notice into Spanish for another, helping another load her belongings into the trunk of my Volvo after her clothes and furniture had been set out on the street. Before she disappeared, I was circling ads in the paper for an apartment closer to the restaurant.

Unintentionally, I got involved in the lives of my staff. Nobody held back in that kitchen. Personal lives were fair game for open discussion, and I couldn't help but be drawn in. I listened to Beth and Candace—sisters struggling with drug addiction, parenthood, and sibling rivalry. After they'd spent too long in a room together, sparks would fly and Beth and Candace would go at it. Suddenly the biggest issue in their lives was which one their mother had loved most. I found myself stepping in. There was no question that I cared about them. I had turned into Susan Lindeborg. She knew that what was going on in our lives could affect our work. Cooking came from a place inside that could be knocked off center by what was happening on the outside.

I was the disciplinarian at home with the girls and encountered similar issues in the kitchen with my staff. There was the morning I came in after a day off. It didn't take me long to notice that the crab cakes were different. Richard had made them, Roshena told me. She couldn't look me in the eye. I knew there was something she wasn't telling me. "Roshena," I said, "what happened with the crab cakes last night?" Richard decided to change the recipe. He wanted to make them the way he did when they were a hit at the Snuggery. He bought a can of Old Bay Seasoning and a jar of Miracle Whip. Without picking out the shells he blended the Old Bay Seasoning and mayonnaise with the jumbo lump. He shaped them into balls and fried them hard in the deep fryer. These were served on my night off. I threw the mixture into the Dumpster and got ready to kill Richard the minute he pushed open the swinging doors to the kitchen. He would be smiling and laughing loudly just as he always was. That's when I'd take the knife out of my back—the very knife he'd stuck into my spine—and disembowel him with it.

When he came in I could tell that someone had tipped him off. I was ready to step in front of him as he swaggered to his locker, grow ten feet tall, and take a big bite out of the top of his head. But here he was coming into the kitchen with his lower lip hanging low and his chin to his chest. The remorseful look on his face reminded me of Magalee. I had caught her with a pair of scissors and Sian's hair all over the floor. When he came closer he looked a little bit like Sian, the time I found where she was playing by following the trail of pearls—left like the bread Hansel and Gretel had dropped—from my grandmother's necklace.

Richard made a mistake. He knew it. What would be the point of killing him now? I remembered when Sian saw the look on my face when I picked up the last pearl. She sobbed the way I wanted to sob. Her little chest was heaving when she crawled into my lap.

Richard was a good cook and a smart guy, but his obsessive need to "improve things" and to try it his way was his downfall. And then there was his Snuggery history. He was perfectly comfortable cooking in this kitchen before I came along. Now we were cooking pork chops in a sauté pan and finishing them in the oven. No matter how much he begged, I didn't let him toss them into the deep fryer to get good and dry and crispy. "No, Richard," I said, shaking my head. "It's faster," he said, holding the pork chop over the bubbling oil. "And this way you know it's done." He thought I was crazy.

Another chef would have insisted he get his white work shirts out of that locker and get out. But I'm a mother. The two most important people in my life have done the unthinkable, and I hoped that my daughters would learn from their mistakes. I did my part by hiding my jewelry box and the scissors. As for Richard, he had already done the worst thing he'd ever do in this kitchen. And I needed him. No one was pounding down the door to work for me. Richard came in on time and took personal pride in making sure the fryer was clean and full of fresh oil. He helped other staff get ready for service. And he was the first to volunteer to come in on the days the kitchen shut down and we scrubbed it from floor to ceiling. I had to put the crab cakes behind us and forgive him.

Did having two children at home make me soft? I preferred to think it made me better able to put my ego aside for the sake of the restaurant. If I fired him he would be swaggering around town claiming I was jealous of his fabulous crab cakes. By keeping him on I hoped he'd be on his toes and every day trying to make it up to me. I didn't have to shout at Richard. Changing the crab cakes—the best seller on the menu—when I wasn't looking probably seemed like a great idea when he was pounding mayonnaise into the delicate lumps of crab. I got him to understand my disappointment that day without raising my voice at all.

There were plenty of times I did shout in the kitchen for the same reason I shouted and punished at home. I cared about my crew and wanted them to get better. If they went on to bigger and better things, as I hoped my children would, I wanted them to be ready and to make beautiful food. I told them, "The food is more important than your feelings." We were in the business of making food and making it perfectly, I told them.

But it was not a job for thin skins, and there were times when leading this team made me think I was losing my mind.

One busy Friday night in August I came up from the basement dry storage room to find that Ronald had left the grill—with a pork chop nearly ablaze.

"Where did Ronald go?" I asked Beth. He had been fidgeting and mumbling to himself most of the evening, but didn't we all when it got this late and this hot? He had mentioned something earlier about an old girlfriend being back in town. He could see her from the open kitchen waving at him from the other side of the huge show window.

Beth looked at me; she was wilting from the heat, her apron wet from perspiration. "That woman out there waving at him. Well . . ." She tossed a salad in a stainless-steel bowl, one hand in a plastic glove. "She did something, bent down or something, out there in front of the window."

I used the tongs to toss the burning pork chop into the pot-and-pan sink. Richard was browning crab cakes in the sauté pan. He chuckled a little to himself, yet he seemed less interested in Ronald leaving the line in the middle of service than Beth. "Chef . . . you haven't heard Ronald complaining that he hasn't gotten any in months?" I'm more than certain my mouth was hanging open. Sure, Ronald had mentioned something. It was all just talk, right? I thought the possibility was remote with Ronald's Coke-bottle glasses, big head, and scrawny coat-hanger body.

Nonetheless, a flash of bare buttocks had made him run out of the kitchen, past the server station, into the dining room, and out the front door. He was probably with that woman in the grass behind the Dumpster. I put another pork chop on the grill.

In my short time as chef at this little neighborhood restaurant, there wasn't much I hadn't seen. I could tell when a staff member was lying. One young lady cried into the phone that her boyfriend had hit her and she couldn't come in. I listened to her sobbing hiccups for about thirty seconds and reminded her that a paycheck would bring her that much closer to leaving his subsidized apartment. She was in an apron and washing lettuce in less than an hour.

Was that new hire really down on her luck? Should I pay her in cash tonight? Will she come back tomorrow? Should I invest valuable training time on her? I got my answer when I noticed her bumming a smoke from a waiter and craning her neck to check out his physical attributes. A lost soul fearing eviction for nonpayment of rent and begging me for $100 at the end of the night is usually so consumed with worry it would take more than "buns of steel" to distract her from her hand-wringing.

I was stronger now and able, no matter what the cost, to exclude anyone who did not conform to our kitchen culture. There were many times when the "tough love" of the kitchen meant I had fired, suspended, or refused to hire someone. On many of these nights, I worked alone. I was a better chef for the experience, better at understanding and building a team. I had seen and managed in the underbelly of the industry. This was not the glamour job of a chef, which I now recognized to be a myth. I was smack-dab in the middle of a subculture of dysfunctional people who worked in the food business and at many of the jobs that employ the working poor.

I owed that first kitchen staff a lot. Wasn't I one of them? My privileged upbringing didn't matter on a Friday night in the heat of busy. And during the day I dealt with some of the same issues that touched members of this struggling staff—a single mother abandoned by an alcoholic husband, struggling to make ends meet. Before taking this better-paying job, I had been working two jobs and rolling pennies from the jar in the girls' room to get enough gas to go to work. The most gratifying part was that whether we faced empty bank accounts, crack habits, or rap sheets, we became the team that made Evening Star Café a success.

ROSHENA'S CHICKEN SALAD

I learned a lot from some of the people who worked for me. With the chicken salad I watched Roshena add a little bit of sugar just before she finished folding in the mayonnaise. It made all the difference.

MAKES ABOUT 10 APPETIZER SERVINGS OR 5 SANDWICHES

ONE 3-TO-4-POUND CHICKEN, ROASTED AND COOLED

½ CUP FINELY DICED SHALLOTS

½ CUP FINELY CHOPPED FLAT-LEAF PARSLEY

1 TABLESPOON SALT

¼ TEASPOON FRESHLY GROUND BLACK PEPPER

1 PINCH CAYENNE PEPPER

1¼ CUPS MAYONNAISE (PREFERABLY HOMEMADE)

JUICE OF 2 LEMONS

¼ CUP SUGAR

Remove the skin and pull the chicken meat off the bone.
Chop and shred the meat with a knife or pulse in a food pro-
cessor. Blend with the remaining ingredients. Refrigerate for
3 or 4 hours before serving.

MUSHROOM AND PEARL ONION RAGOUT

This sauce is so easy to make and can transform the
most ordinary cut of meat into something extraordinary.

MAKES ENOUGH SAUCE FOR 6 SERVINGS

2 TABLESPOONS PURE OLIVE OIL

I POUND SHIITAKE MUSHROOMS, STEMMED AND QUARTERED

I POUND CREMINI MUSHROOMS, STEMMED AND QUARTERED

I POUND WHITE PEARL ONIONS, PEELED AND BLANCHED

1/2 CUP DRY SHERRY

I CUP HEAVY CREAM

SALT AND PEPPER TO TASTE

Heat the oil in a skillet over high heat until just smoking. Add
the mushrooms and toss until they are softened and begin-
ning to brown. As the mushrooms start to release their water,
continue to cook them, stirring occasionally over medium
heat until the water is evaporated and they begin to brown
further. Add the onions and cook for another 2 or 3 minutes.
Add the sherry and bring the mixture to a boil. Turn the heat
down to low and add the cream. Let the mixture simmer for

10 minutes, or until the cream is reduced by more than half. Season with salt and pepper. Serve with a roasted flank steak or even a simple Salisbury steak.

THE BEST MASHED POTATOES ANYWHERE

The key is ice-cold water and cold potatoes. Make sure they are really firm and free of blemishes while you're peeling them.

MAKES ABOUT 8 SERVINGS

11 IDAHO POTATOES, PEELED AND WASHED

1 CUP MILK

2 CUPS HEAVY CREAM

1/2 CUP BUTTER

SALT AND PEPPER

In a large and heavy pot, cover the potatoes in very cold water. Bring them to a boil over high heat. While the potatoes are boiling, set a saucepan with the milk, cream, and butter on the stove indirectly over the heat so that the butter melts and the cream is warmed. Continue cooking the potatoes until a knife slides easily through the thickest part of the potato. If you can pick up the potato with the knife, the cooked potato should slide off and fall back into the boiling water. Once they are cooked run the potatoes, three at a time, through a food mill into a bowl. The milled potatoes should be light and crumbly and resemble grains of rice. Work quickly and do not allow the potatoes to cool. With a rubber spatula, gradually blend in the warm milk and butter mixture. Add salt and pepper to taste. Serve immediately.

HOUSE-MADE MAYONNAISE

I've never been a big fan of mayonnaise. For that reason I use really good olive oil, fresh eggs, and more lemon juice than makes sense.

MAKES 6 CUPS OF MAYONNAISE

7 EGG YOLKS

JUICE OF 3 LEMONS

1 TEASPOON SALT

1/4 TEASPOON FRESHLY GROUND BLACK PEPPER

1 CUP PURE OLIVE OIL

4 TO 5 CUPS VEGETABLE OIL

Whisk the yolks and lemon juice together with the salt and pepper. Slowly whisk in the olive oil and then the vegetable oil until the mayonnaise is very thick.

Three

FOOD EQUALS LOVE TO A
WOULD-BE CHEF

How many of us can pinpoint the origins of our addictions? Does the nymphomaniac recollect at what point in time sex, and lots of it, became the source of her comfort and security? Does the kleptomaniac remember when that first pilfered item brought all calm? And what about the alcoholic? Is there one particular moment that can be referred to as the beginning of the end?

Looking back, I know exactly when food came to be important to me. I sat in the kitchen while my father sweated onions. I read the recipes in magazines and studied the glossy pictures of the finished product. Food to me was more than just the raw ingredients heated together. It was a symbol of love and caring. I was one of those kids in kindergarten who accessorized with a length of yarn and a bright brass key. My earliest memory of my parents caring for me was the lunch that waited for me in the fridge.

In 1969 we moved from Westbury to Great Neck, New

York. My mother was hoping that her five children would continue their education past high school. Great Neck, with 365 high-school seniors headed to college, painted a better picture of our future than the high school from the old neighborhood that had two seniors ready to matriculate.

We rented a two-bedroom apartment on Wooleys Lane, about a fifteen-minute walk to Clover Drive Elementary School, until my parents could scrape up enough cash to put something down on what would eventually be my childhood home. The half-day kindergarten was over by 12:15. So while my brothers and sisters stayed until 3:00, I made the walk back home to Wooleys Lane alone.

The loop of yarn was long enough for me to unlock the dead bolt without taking the key from around my neck. Once the heavy steel door creaked open, I stood in the eerie quiet of being home alone. There were the smells of home—my father's aftershave, instant coffee, and the faux leather sofa; then there were the mysterious creaks and groans that came from the walls and floorboards. None of these things are appreciated so much as when you come home alone.

I'd turn on *The Price Is Right* to drown out the groans—"Just the building settling," my mother would tell me when she called. Then I made my way to the dining room. There were usually seven of us at the big walnut laminate round on a white steel pedestal, overlooked by the still-life painting of figs. But at lunchtime during the week, I found the table set for one and a note from my father. "It's tuna today. Pour yourself a glass of milk. There's fruit in the refrigerator. Love, Daddy."

I didn't feel so "home alone" now. The empty apartment with its stark white walls and picture windows looking out onto busy Middle Neck Road was suddenly warmer. My lunch was carefully prepared; the sandwich was neatly cut into two triangles, and the two oatmeal cookies crowded the bone-white saucer. My tall glass stood empty and waiting for me to fill it with milk. The glossy red apple was there in the fridge, just as Daddy said it would be.

Here was love and thoughtfulness on the table. Food was the most perfect form of love, I thought. It could be reliable, comforting, and satisfying. Sometimes there was too much mayonnaise with the bologna or too many brown spots on the banana. That was okay. My waiting lunch meant I was not for-gotten. Though they were not there, Daddy and Mommy would take care of me.

The table set for one in the middle of the day in the quiet apartment at first chased a head-pounding loneliness. When I got used to this solitary lunch, I started looking at it as the sin-gular attention with which the youngest of five is rarely hon-ored. I felt special. It was my name on the note my father left in his large block letters. Lunch was often one of my father's favorites: liverwurst with butter and onions, a lunch only he and I would dare eat. It was a bond between us, and my first in-troduction to the power of food.

From that point on I wasn't just interested in food, I was fascinated by it. I would spend my evenings sitting on a stool in the kitchen watching my father reduce a chicken to its parts or hammer a coconut open for its milk and flesh to put into the rice. My father usually lost the fifteen-minute argu-ment over whether he or my mother would be at the stove. It puzzled me that they both considered it a chore after eight hours behind a desk.

I marveled at the confidence and know-how with which my father, and occasionally my mother, approached the task. He'd run his knife across the smooth rock he'd found long ago in the yard and chop just the right amount of onion. With the precision of a surgeon, he'd close up the just-stuffed turkey cavity. Here was also a man whose sense of humor could begin and end in the kitchen. As he scraped the last caramelized bit of sauce or crunchy coating of breading from the bottom of the pan, he'd recite one of his favorites: "If you cook the way you walk, give me the bottom of the pot. The bottom is the best part. . . ."

His skill and work did not go unappreciated. The call to dinner would get the rest of the household out of a book and away from the TV. Vigorous and hasty hand washing would ensue and the jumps down the stairs would rattle the wall hangings.

Surely my father had to realize that by simmering those pork chops in mushroom gravy, or coating those pieces of chicken in lemon zest and bread crumbs, he had silenced and amazed five teenagers. For that half an hour while forks and knives made sparks and we were often reduced to arguing and begging for more, that man—who had taught himself to cook while his mother fretted after an unfaithful, then finally invalid husband—was the most important person on earth. I noticed. And as a young teen, I was determined to enjoy that power and attention myself.

I was the youngest of five. At school and at home, my little voice was often not heard. And with two working parents, it was difficult getting attention.

I put down the Tolstoy and studied one of my father's

cookbooks. I decided on an adaptation of something I considered awe inspiring, and that I still make today. The recipe was suitably complicated, but not too exotic. And on that night, as on more nights to follow (by the time I was thirteen I had learned to stretch a floured bedsheet over the dining room table and was pulling my own strudel dough) I was the youngest of five children who often went all evening with her nose in a book and without saying a word. When I put dinner on the table, I got everyone's attention.

Before long I was tackling the bread recipes on the back of the flour bag. I ordered the booklet by sending in three proofs of purchase from Fleischmann's yeast so I could learn the secrets of English muffins and pita bread. There were recipes everywhere, all waiting to be conquered. Before high-school graduation I had quite a repertoire: lemon pound cake, peanut brittle, and pickled young cucumbers picked from our garden next to the garage.

When I got married I was twenty-one and maybe a little too anxious to play house. My skill in the kitchen had made me popular with college roommates; certainly it would be something my husband would brag about at the office. So I took the usual path to a man's heart. But it felt as if I wasn't making any headway. While I wrestled the lobsters for the lobster Newburg I served on our first anniversary, my young husband, Hakim, was wrestling his own demons. Later I found that he was self-medicating the demons into silence by washing down Valium, Xanax, or Benadryl capsules with Wild Turkey. Like many of my efforts in the kitchen, the lobster Newburg dinner and the chocolate truffles on Valentine's Day made just a ripple. The wine that accompanied dinner was always a huge success, as was the sherry for the sauce or the brandy in the glaze.

There were nights when he claimed he was working late and I blew out the candles and ate seafood crepes, Dover sole, or stuffed shoulder of veal by myself. It was like being in the apartment on Wooleys Lane again. The floorboards creaked and I waited with whoever was on television for the door to swing open. Maybe I was just missing the house full of eaters that made mealtime an event.

I started making less and less time for kitchen circus acts as I moved up the corporate ladder. I was working late at the office now, too. Why hurry home? Sometimes I'd stop for a drink or grab a pizza with friends from the office. I'd put the key in the door, thinking maybe I'd find him waiting for me for a change. But no, the sparsely furnished living room was tomb dark and quiet. There were the distractions of deadlines and meetings in Chicago. With every promotion I made the necessary change in my appearance. I got busy with hair and nail appointments, and I spent hours at the department store looking for new pumps and smart suits. Food was placed on a back burner until the baby came.

I'm sure every new parent feels that rush. From you a perfect little being has sprung. Wow, what could be more incredible than that? Sure, it was even exhilarating to make food for her with my own body and equipment that I'd been walking around with all of these years. But soon that wasn't enough. I watched little teeth spring out of her gums and confessed to little Maga-lee that I wanted nothing more than to make her something to eat. Pediatricians nowadays go by different rules than when I was a kid. "Cereal only after four months," he said. "You can begin the carrots after six." That was agony. I had to find the simple joy of watching her enjoy carrots and then the simple things like peanut butter. Maybe I was too cautious. Afraid of gas and colic, I avoided sauces and onions when feeding Magalee. To this day she is wary of both. Sian, on the other hand, was a thumb sucker. The cayenne-coated nail polish from the drugstore was her first introduction to spicy food and started her love of anything with jalapeño. No one is as careful with their second child, and I fed Sian with much less caution.

I finally had my audience. When I burnt the toast they noticed. When the applesauce came out really good, I was rewarded with appreciative giggles and clean plates. My love for kitchen magic was coming back, thanks to the children. Maternity leave gave me time and I started cooking again. Big family dinners with homemade rolls, blueberry muffins, and elaborate cakes covered with ganache. I'd call friends and neighbors to come and help us grill and eat the whole red snapper from the fish market. When the kids were ready for school and day care I reluctantly went back to work, eventually phasing out the nine-to-five to work at home.

When Sian was almost two, I traded my briefcase for a set of culinary-school-issued J.A. Henckels knives. My family and friends were active and sometimes unknowing participants when I was doing homework or practicing at home what Pascal or François had shown me in cooking school. I served them sweetbreads in a sauce of capers and didn't tell them until their plates were clean what they had eaten. Soon there was duck confit in the potpie, and osso buco in the braise.

I could get them talking or stun them into awed silence

with what was on their plates. I could even lure a reluctant babysitter with smells from the oven.

There was increasing evidence that my children were talking about their meals at school. Sian would break the silence while we waited to cross the street with something like, "Mommy, some of the kids in my class didn't know you can eat squid." Or Magalee would silently slide her lunch box onto the kitchen counter. I'd have to ask her about the glum look on her face. "I was trying to tell them that the bread in my sandwich was shaped funny because it's challah. The whole cafeteria laughed at me."

Not long after that I discovered the importance of food to my young children. While it had become a way for me to express myself, to communicate what I felt was important, and to earn a living, for them it was a status symbol, a way to relate to others, a form of socialization, a glimpse and clue to who they are.

The revealing display on the table at the cafeteria provided a window into the life of a schoolmate worth hundreds of questions and thousands of playdates. Was your mother generous? Did she let you eat candy? Did she take the time to make your lunch or were you the one with the Lunchables every day? Did you eat weird stuff out of Tupperware? Was there nothing but vegetables and sensible things? Or did she throw in a surprise every now and then—a piece of cake or some Hershey's Kisses?

While I wasn't that unlucky kid who was ridiculed for "stinking up" the cafeteria with a turn of my thermos, I do recall having to explain to the kids in my cafeteria at school why I was neatly folding my brown paper bag to bring my lunch in it again tomorrow. "I'm a conservationist," I replied seriously, as my father had coached me. Five lunch-size brown paper bags were hard to come by. If I was lucky and got the thick and sturdy one that the supermarket used to keep the ice cream from wetting the other groceries, I was certain to conserve my lunch bag for at least two weeks.

There were many defining moments for my girls in elementary school, and none of them were as crucial as the daily tests in the cafeteria. Sian, although she ate squid on occasion, was a normal red-blooded American preschooler. Magalee, despite the fact that her sandwich was made with bread that required her to clear her throat to pronounce, really was not as odd as one might have thought.

Even to the girls, food was more than just a way to get past hunger. While a student in cooking school and a young cook, I learned to take advantage of this to influence their school careers. By the time I was leading kitchens, and soon a restaurant of my own, I was able to use food and cooking to teach and correct behavior and give positive reinforcement.

There was power in food. I wasn't alone in feeling this. I knew it was true when I was young and left kindergarten for my lunch alone in an empty apartment. When I watched as my father thrilled us with pineapple upside-down cake and "ruined" Thanksgiving by trying a new recipe for stuffing that called for orange zest instead of pork sausage, I knew that we were all in touch with that power in one form or another.

Food had become important to me because of all of these things. Now, convinced it was important to my children, I planned to use it as the focal point of happy and healthy childhoods—to help me raise them to be healthy, happy, and responsible adults, and to encourage them to continue to see food as more than just nourishment, but as part of their identity and a continuing life lesson.

There had to be more to raising children than spankings and groundings. As complex and unpredictable as children can be, the parental response to their behavior is not always simple. My response characteristically included the lecture and revocation of privileges. But it was never without a recipe.

The earliest lesson in giving from the kitchen came for Magalee on Valentine's Day. Her second-grade class celebrated by handing each other those little heart-clad cards in envelopes. Magalee and I decided she'd bring in heart-shaped sugar cookies. We'd write the names of her classmates on the cookies with chocolate. Even the teacher was thrilled to get this personalized, edible Valentine. It has become a tradition for the girls. They are both old enough now to manage their Valentine's Day tradition with very little help from me. The cookies are allowed to cool and then stacked with layers of parchment paper in flat plastic containers. On Valentine's Day the girls are more careful boarding the bus with their cookies than when it's the day of the science fair.

SUGAR COOKIES WITH CHOCOLATE ICING

This is simply the cookie for every occasion. For Christmas we cut them into star shapes and frost them red and green—confectioners' sugar, water, and food coloring.

MAKES 2 DOZEN COOKIES

THE COOKIES

3 1/2 CUPS FLOUR

1/4 TEASPOON SALT

1 TEASPOON BAKING POWDER

1 CUP UNSALTED BUTTER, AT ROOM TEMPERATURE

1 1/2 CUPS SUGAR

2 LARGE EGGS

GRATED ZEST OF 1 ORANGE

A PINCH OF FRESHLY GRATED NUTMEG

2 TEASPOONS PURE VANILLA EXTRACT

THE CHOCOLATE ICING

1 CUP MILK CHOCOLATE CHIPS

1 SQUEEZE BOTTLE WITH SMALL TIP

In a bowl whisk together the flour, salt, and baking powder. Set aside.

In the bowl of a stand mixer beat the butter and sugar until light and fluffy (3 to 4 minutes). Add the eggs, zest, nutmeg, and vanilla extract and beat until combined. Add the flour mixture and beat until you have a smooth dough.

Divide the dough in half and wrap each half in plastic wrap. Refrigerate it for about 1 hour, or until firm enough to roll.

Preheat the oven to 350 degrees and place the rack in the center of the oven. Line two baking sheets with parchment paper.

Remove one half of the chilled dough from the refrigerator and, on a lightly floured surface, roll out the dough to a thickness of ¼ inch. Keep turning the dough as you roll, making sure the dough does not stick to the counter or board. Cut out desired shapes using a lightly floured cookie cutter, and transfer the cookies to the prepared baking sheets. Place the baking sheets with the unbaked cookies in the refrigerator for 10 to 15 minutes to chill the dough, which prevents the cookies from spreading and losing their shape while baking.

Place the chilled sheet of cookies in the oven on the center rack. They should begin to brown at the edges in about 10 minutes. Remove the cookies from the oven and let them cool on the tray for five minutes. Using a stiff metal spatula, carefully lift the cookies off the sheet and place them on a parchment-lined cutting board. Let cool.

Melt the milk chocolate chips in a stainless-steel bowl over a pot of simmering water. Transfer the warm melted chocolate into the squeeze bottle. Keep a bowl of warm water nearby should the chocolate start to cool and thicken. Using the squeeze bottle like a fountain pen, write names on each cookie. Cursive works better than print as it is difficult to stop the flow of chocolate from the squeeze bottle. Cover the tip of the squeeze bottle with your finger to keep chocolate from dripping once you've written each name. Let the cookies cool for 30 minutes before moving them.

DADDY'S TUNA SALAD

All of the components of my father's recipe come together into the perfect tuna salad sandwich. This is

just one of those tastes that stays with you. Best served on
a good sturdy white bread.

MAKES ABOUT 3 SANDWICHES

1 CAN OF TUNA PACKED IN WATER, DRAINED WELL

2 HARD-BOILED EGGS, CUT INTO CUBES

1 TABLESPOON PICKLE RELISH

2 TABLESPOONS FINELY MINCED ONION

3 TO 5 HEAPING TABLESPOONS HELLMANN'S OR BEST FOODS
MAYONNAISE (DEPENDING ON YOUR TASTE)

SALT AND PEPPER

Stir the first four ingredients together using a fork. Then fold
in the mayonnaise and salt and pepper to taste. Refrigerate
overnight. Garnish with Boston lettuce and a thinly sliced
tomato.

STUFFED ONIONS WITH ONION GRAVY

For my debut at the family stove I wanted to make
something that my father had never made before.
I have to admit I was showing off. It might have
earned me a punch in the arm from one of my four
brothers and sisters. On this night I learned I could
show off with food without earning the pride-suppressing
retribution of rival siblings.

MAKES 10 FIRST-COURSE OR

5 MAIN-COURSE SERVINGS

THE ONIONS AND FILLING

10 MEDIUM ONIONS

3 TABLESPOONS BUTTER

2 TEASPOONS FRESH THYME LEAVES, FINELY MINCED

2 POUNDS COOKED PORK OR LAMB (YESTERDAY'S ROAST WILL DO),
CUT INTO VERY FINE CUBES

2 TEASPOONS SALT

1/2 TEASPOON PEPPER

1/4 CUP FRESH BREAD CRUMBS

THE SAUCE

2 TABLESPOONS BUTTER

3 OR 4 ONIONS, DICED

1/3 CUP CHICKEN STOCK

1/2 CUP WHITE WINE OR DRY SHERRY

SALT AND PEPPER

THE TOPPING

1 CUP FRESH BREAD CRUMBS

1/4 CUP BUTTER, MELTED

3 TABLESPOONS CHOPPED FLAT-LEAF PARSLEY

*Peel and carefully trim the 10 onions. Cut the tops to expose
the expanse of rings. Trim the hairy root off the bottom but
leave the root end intact so the onion has a flat bottom but
stays together. Place the onions in a heavy, deep saucepan
with a lid, and pour in water to a depth that immerses the
onions halfway. Simmer them, covered, over medium heat
for about 20 minutes. You should be able to stick a sharp*

knife into the center of the onions with ease. Do not over-cook them or they'll fall apart while you're scooping out the flesh. Let the onions cool on a platter. Using a melon baller or grapefruit spoon, scoop out the insides of the onions. You should leave about three layers of onion in each one. Reserve the inside pulp and set aside for the sauce.

While the pulp is cooling, melt the butter over low heat and add the thyme. Add the pork or lamb and cook over low heat, stirring constantly. Add the salt, pepper, and bread crumbs. Simmer until almost dry (about another 5 minutes). Transfer to a bowl and allow to cool.

While the filling is cooling, make the sauce: Melt the butter in a saucepan. Add the diced onions and cook until very soft; do not brown. Pour the chicken stock over the onions. Add the reserved onion pulp and cook off as much liquid as possible before adding the wine or sherry. Reduce over medium heat for about 3 more minutes. Transfer this mixture to a blender and purée. Season with salt and pepper to taste. Keep warm.

Preheat the oven to 425 degrees. Fill the onions with 2 or 3 tablespoons of the filling. Go ahead and pile it high. The effect of the stuffing swelling out of the onions after you've baked them is the effect you want. Place the onions pretty close together in a buttered deep baking pan. An 11 × 6 × 2-inch Pyrex casserole is perfect. Mix the bread crumbs, melted butter, and chopped parsley for the topping. Sprinkle this mixture over the onions. Bake for 30 to 40 minutes, or until heated through and browned.

Spoon some sauce on a plate and top it with 2 of the onions for a main course, or 1 for a fine first course. A wild rice blend and some green beans are good accompaniments.

Four

STRIVING FOR PERFECTION IN AN IMPERFECT WORLD

A year before the divorce was final, I received a package at Evening Star Café from my attorney. It was the separation agreement. I had full custody and the sailboat. He got restricted visitation and the RV. It needed to be signed and notarized. I took a break from deveining shrimp and pulling the guts out of squid. Good press at Evening Star Café meant the secret was out. It also meant ten pounds more shrimp and fifteen pounds more squid.

We met at the old house on Third Street. Years ago, before Magalee was born, we bit our nails and subsisted on bag lunches and buttered pasta to save the ten-thousand-dollar down payment. It was heading toward twilight and I could see the last of the sunlight making the yellow roses in the backyard glow. I remembered how many weekends I'd dedicated to wrestling aphids and drought. I put up a good fight but in the summer of 1987 I lost the rhododendrons. The roses, planted in the 1940s, had endured. We spent weekends stripping paint and wallpaper in this building that had been our home for nine years. Now the house belonged to the bank and it seemed a neutral enough place to sign the separation agreement.

I didn't know that my estranged husband, Hakim, would arrive armed. He was loaded with the latest psychobabble about what makes people drink and take drugs. He predicted that Sian would definitely spend a night in a gutter sometime in her future. And living with me—a classic enabler—might mean Magalee would suffer a similar fate. According to my soon-to-be-ex-husband I had enabled him straight to the liquor store. Chugging those malt liquors in the car before coming in to dinner was what he had to do after spending a few hours in my company. Of course my tendency to enable would affect my daughters in the same way.

My mother didn't have as dire a prediction. She worried about the revolving door of babysitters. Surely Rachel's gum chewing would rub off, and they'd take to bleaching their hair like Leslie. Never mind that Valerie was attending American University on a full scholarship or that Eileen was leaving us to join AmeriCorps. The girls would be chewing gum and bleaching their hair and walking the streets at night to earn a living. Being a cook was no way for a single mother to make a living. It was selfish of me. Weren't my parents home and there for me every night?

While I didn't really believe that my daughters would be gum-chewing bourbon drinkers, I did feel that the pressure was on. I have to admit that I was tough on them. It wasn't enough for them to just go to school every day. They had to get straight As. I wanted them to be perfect—better than perfect. Surviving as children parented by a single mother who cooked for a living wasn't good enough. They had to be well behaved, brilliant, play the viola and the harp, and recite Shakespeare.

I wanted to prove I had the parenting skills and drive to make them the children every parent wished they'd had. I wanted Magalee to perform a viola solo at every concert, and then get the lead in the school play. And Sian, she had to bring home the biggest magazine-cover pumpkin from the October field trip to the farm. The harp would be easy for young Sian. Sure, she had to learn the piano first. Not a problem.

As much as I tried to shake off the criticism from folks who didn't approve of my attempting to single-parent while working as a chef, it did set little voices of guilt off in my head. We weren't like everyone else's family. The little kid conversations about sitting with Mommy and Daddy in front of the TV just weren't part of my offspring's vernacular. I wasn't there for the PTA meetings. It was the babysitter at the playdates and behind them on the swings in the park. Most of their friends' mothers had never met me.

I felt guilty for not being there when they were home and needed help with homework or to be tucked in at night. I was afraid of missing important moments in their lives. And I missed being with them. I insisted the babysitters save any tooth that slipped out, and gave them explicit nighttime instructions so that the tired "tooth fairy," wearing big work boots and fumbling around with cut fingers or burns, would suffer no surprises in the dark.

I wanted them to be happy despite the decisions that I'd made. Our lives were different now. I hoped for the best. Maybe it didn't look like it right now, but I pictured our life as a house being renovated. Certainly we were in for some ugly times with plaster dust and drop cloths—but soon there'd be fresh paint and new carpeting.

Raising perfect children isn't easy when you live a normal life. But when you're just starting out in the demanding food-service industry and working nights and weekends, it's tantamount to spinning plates. Throw in an absent father making and breaking promises, and those plates I was spinning were on fire and I was also riding a unicycle in a puddle of gasoline.

Keeping my word with my children and doing for them what I promised and letting them know when I couldn't make it to the school play or the field trip was well within my control. But I found myself doing the unthinkable to keep their little-girl faces from sinking into heart-wrenching frowns. I quietly stepped in when their absent father disappointed them. I found myself covering up for their father's failings. I made excuses when he didn't show up for his scheduled visits. Sian was a smart four-year-old. "What's today, Mommy?" she asked when I met her outside of her classroom. She couldn't possibly remember that her father had called last month and said that he would be in town by the time school was out that day.

"Today's the nineteenth, honey. Why?"

"Oh, nothing." Did she know?

On another day, Magalee was sitting on the steps waiting for the mailman. There were photos from a July Fourth visit her father had promised to send. Now it was October. Even Leonard the mailman was out of excuses. I was the one who quietly placed the Dracula fangs on Magalee's pillow that he said he'd send in time for her Halloween costume. At the time, I was afraid she'd ask, "Mommy, where'd those teeth come from?" And just as I had feared, I had to confess that I had bought them.

There was no hiding it; I couldn't protect them from him. Their own father was bent on being a fly in the ointment. He was determined to bring down my smiling, happy, perfect children.

And of course it would be all my fault. When he did show up at last, he'd bring gifts—not the ones he'd promised, but no matter. No matter what had transpired—the forgotten pictures, the no-shows—they still ran to the door shouting "Daddy, Daddy!" He was made of Teflon. It was as if the clown from the circus were at our house. They laughed louder and didn't get sleepy at ten o'clock. I had to make them go to bed. I played the role of spoilsport and villain. After he was gone, I was the one left to tell them, "No," "Do your homework," "Eat your broccoli." I was the one left to sit alone on the sofa staring at the blurry newspaper print, listening to the pillow-muffled sobs through the closed bedroom door after I'd punished one of them.

They didn't know or care that I fought him constantly for nonpayment of child support. He claimed he could only afford fifty dollars a month. Health insurance, school supplies, rent, and clothes for two growing children ate up my paycheck. I watched Hakim light a cigarette as he walked to his car at the end of his visit. He might as well have been burning five-dollar bills. When I did get the courts to enforce an increase, he suddenly became unemployed. Still, I was determined to keep a stiff upper lip. On my night off after the girls went to bed, I repaired the holes in my socks and chef pants, rolled pennies for gas money, and made sure they had five dollars for the field trip to Ford's Theatre.

·   ·   ·

As chef of Evening Star Café I was suffering my own inconsistencies with positive and negative reinforcement. I went to work and worked harder than I ever imagined I could. There were busy weekend nights when everything that had been prepped that morning and afternoon was gone by 9:00 P.M. One of my most vivid memories is of a customer holding a bowl of white corn chowder to her lips and scraping what was clinging to the bowl into her mouth. As I watched her I felt like a success. I started to understand that the power that came in the ingredients I put together extended beyond my family's clean plates. The press was good and the customers were filling the dining room, patio, and bar the minute we opened.

There was blood and sweat in that kitchen, but the exhaustion often gave way to jokes and laughter. We all knew what Friday and Saturday meant. More clean towels were stacked at stations, knives were taken to the steel, and aprons were tied on tighter. Friday and Saturday meant six cups of rice for eight gallons of gumbo. The chickens were started to roast at 4:00 P.M. and then we threw ten more chickens in the oven at 7:00. The roasted chicken was so popular that there were some nights we didn't get the second round of chicken into the oven early enough. We'd run out before 7:00. Irritated and disappointed, servers would throw their pads down on the quarry tile. Customers would ask to see the menu again; I could see the frowning, dejected faces from the open kitchen. Grown men and women sad and certain they would not get past this disappointment. As if Christmas weren't coming after all.

The team in the kitchen took failure seriously. There was guilt and blame tossed about on nights like those—when busy spun us out of control. At the end of the night we wore the

OUT OF THE FRYING PAN

scars of battle. Sharing the suffering of Saturday night forged a team.

But I had to endure Sunday. I had to endure Sunday alone. We did an average brunch, occasionally getting backed up on the pecan waffles that took six minutes in the single waffle iron, but I could handle that because I had Sunday night off. When the last customer was gone and the kitchen was cleaned and the night shift was given instructions for dinner service, I was ready to go. I hadn't seen my daughters all week. This was my five hours with them—dinner, quiet time, and a bedtime story—an important five hours for all three of us.

Then came the meetings. It started with an owners' brunch in the bar that quickly turned into a gripe session. Pens and pads were brought out. Before I had completely dried my hands I was called in to join them at the table. The three owners faced me at the dimly lit back table near the bar. They were rested and well fed. I was sticky with food and sweat and a little wobbly after the second half of my Saturday night–Sunday morning turnaround.

During that first meeting, the list took up about twenty lines on the yellow legal pad. Things like, "We need more sandwich options at lunch" or "Is there any way to keep from running out of chicken?" But the meetings continued each successive Sunday, and they were chewing up my five hours. I answered quickly, reading the list over their shoulders, and skipping to item number fifteen. Swore I could answer items nine through thirteen with two sentences. Did we really need a prep cook every day? Why did I yell at the servers so much? How come Richard can't run the kitchen on my night off as well as I can? As the weeks wore on the meetings became ugly.

Maybe my fatigue made me appear nonchalant and uncaring. My answers were flip and inadequate. The list turned into a character assessment and a detailed description of how I wasn't doing my job. "Do you really expect us to believe that you're working ninety-hour weeks?" "What difference does it make if we have a table of eighteen? Isn't that just like having nine tables of two?" "You're resisting the financial success of the restaurant." Sunday after Sunday, watching as my five hours ticked down, I tried for the quick "resolution" by just agreeing to everything. In and outside of the kitchen, I was taking a beating.

It was as if I were hanging on to a swaying skyscraper. Like so many new chefs I was anxious to succeed and make a name for myself. I had made the fatal mistake of falling in love with my kitchen. I designed it. I created it. It was my first. I could not deny my attachment to the tile and stainless steel. The clatter of finished plates hitting, then sliding on the shelf under the heat lamp, the happy customers thrilled to meet me, and watching the bread swipes through traces of sauce on returning dishes set my heart to racing.

I became convinced I was working for lunatics. The crowded dining room and the *mise en place* backed up in eight-quart containers each night led me to believe that some things must have been going right. The reviewers were raving, now that we'd hit our stride. How come the owners were so down on me? Hadn't I taken this shoestring-budget kitchen and misfit staff and done better than anyone could have anticipated?

One evening I was able to escape the restaurant shortly after 9:00 P.M. A regular customer had been in with all of her women friends to celebrate her birthday. "Join us for my cake," she insisted. I drove through the dark streets of one of the richest neighborhoods in Alexandria. I was in my work boots and chef pants but was able to find a clean T-shirt to throw on.

I sat down around the table with all of these women dripping in Saks Fifth Avenue and Tiffany's and enjoying champagne and carrot cake (the best I'd ever had, I told the hostess). When her husband came in after a late night at the office (an attorney for the Environmental Protection Agency), she introduced him to the gathering around the table. "Honey, this is Suzanne; she works with Betsy at the high school." He nodded and smiled, but his mind was still on the papers in his desk and the contents of his briefcase. "You remember Katherine Stuart," she continued, "of the Marblehead Stuarts." He smiled his vacant smile at Kate. "And I'm not sure you've been formerly introduced but you know her work." I stood as she gestured her ring-heavy hand my way. "This is Gillian, the chef at Evening Star." At this the husband exclaimed, "What!," put down his briefcase, and let his overcoat slide to the floor as he vigorously shook my hand. Being a chef gave me, a poor girl from Long Island, instant status. To my customers I was a celebrity.

As hard as it was, and as demoralizing at times, I refused to give up. I had something to prove to my ex-husband, to my family, and to the chefs who'd trained me—and now, to the owners. But though I appreciated the recognition from my customer and her husband, nothing raised my spirits and the strength to face another day better than the phone call. "Guilliaahn!" the caller shouted. It was a familiar French accent that I couldn't place. "Annie told me you were in the magazine." It was Alain Lecomte, the chef from my first cooking job at the vineyard. His English had really improved, although he had stomped about the kitchen in his clogs, refusing to take the classes that the vineyard was paying for. "Congratulations"—then something in French—"I mean, I am very happy for you. You do good things at this Even Ning Stah, no?"

Boy, did that feel good. What a way to start my week. I could face anything now, even an empty walk-in, truckloads of inventory to put away by myself, and shorthanded day and evening shifts. The phone call took away precious minutes but it was worth it. I hurried to decide on a soup of the day and, without any thought of the outcome, peeled a half case of carrots (horse chokers as they are known in the business) into my biggest pot with a few onions, wine, and water. I was in such a hurry the carrots weren't fully cooked when I ran the soup through the blender. I added cream and tossed in something to make it interesting—sage. This became the most requested soup of the day in the history of my cooking for a living.

The positive reinforcement from a chef I worked for so long ago and for so short a time was a real boost. I put my head down and got my work done and realized it all really wasn't about me. The stress and anxiety that boiled over on Sunday afternoons was what the Meeting of the Yellow Legal Pad was all about. I didn't have access to the bank records, but I'm sure as money rolled in and quickly slid out, my anxious bosses were grasping at whatever they thought would amount to more black and less red. Sometimes, although they had no way of knowing it, you couldn't do a thing except wait and be patient. Moreover, they had plans. There was the purchase of the building and plans for another location on the drawing board.

The unexpected pat on the back did wonders for me, and I thought about how much pressure I might have been putting on my daughters. I didn't stop pushing them to succeed, but I did consciously give them more opportunities to play and express themselves on their own terms. And more praise came out of me. What I couldn't control was their father and how he treated them. The best I could do was to make sure they knew that it wasn't about them. Like me, they were dealing with someone else's fear.

And it could be toxic. I eventually had to leave Evening Star. Soon the owners' fear seeped into the kitchen, spilled onto the stove, and was ruining the plates. On my night off someone went out to buy sugar snap peas to add to the sauté of root vegetables flanking my winter pork chop. "There's no green on the plate," they said. The properly cooked, rested, and sliced breast of duck was being stopped at the kitchen door. "Are you sure that's cooked enough?" one of the owners exclaimed, stopping the server before he could make it to the table.

It took me about a year to realize that I didn't have to stick around for this. Cooking for a living is hard enough without playing dodgeball at the same time.

My school-age children had become members of a restaurant family now that I was a single mother working as a chef. Child care was always my biggest concern. There was a scramble to find a replacement when Becky moved to Wisconsin to finish her Ph.D. Issues and incidents such as when Valerie had choir practice and Tina couldn't start until Wednesday meant the kids were often at the restaurant with me, doing their homework in my office off the kitchen or down in the basement watching a video. These two hadn't reached their teenage years, yet they were exposed to more adults and more personalities than I had been at their tender age.

There were students, recovering alcoholics, struggling artists, ex-convicts, teachers, social workers, high-school dropouts, drug addicts, hard workers, lazy slobs, and more; all of whom my daughters were taught to address politely with a Hello, how are you?

Did some of these personalities prove contagious? Is that what caused my daughters to exhibit behavior that I could not understand? Is every mother confronted with the sudden attempt by her children to "be someone" whether we like the model they've chosen or not? No matter how often we lay out the path and litter the road with characteristics and traits and codes that we deem worthy, how is it that they make a three-point turn and choose to emulate the lazy slob who gets shouted at every night at work, or to express their deep admiration for the high-school dropout?

It was the third week of kindergarten when Sian came home with a faux pearl necklace and "ruby" earrings the size of half-dollars clipped to her tiny lobes. She stretched her neck out and raised her chin, tilting her head slightly to the right. The jewels caught the last bit of sunlight and glowed. "Wow," her sister said, stopping in her tracks. "Where'd you get those earrings, Sian?"

"Ms. Evans thought I looked good in them so she let me have them," Sian said, puckering her lips slightly and extending her bony arm so that we could see the marcasite cocktail ring.

Sian was wearing her weakness: the trappings of femininity that I barely wore now in my new career. She and her sister had long since raided my old jewelry box of those medals of conquest and salary increase, but they no longer held their interest.

But let a friend walk in with a Tiffany watch or a gold chain or dangling earrings and Sian would approach her, eyes trans-fixed, saliva gathering in the corners of her mouth. She'd squeeze her hands together behind her back, perhaps to con-tain herself from reaching out and grabbing. "I like your neck-lace," she'd say softly.

Magalee had developed a healthy suspicion of just about everyone. "Ms. Evans gave them to you? Yeah, right!"

And Sian had learned to defend herself no matter how ridiculous the lie. "Yes, she did. Honest."

The next morning, with red face and pouting lips, Sian poured the baubles into Ms. Evans's hands. She was thanked for her honesty and admired for her courage in returning the "missing" jewelry. I forbade Sian to play in the class costume box, yet checked her backpack regularly.

I had to think back to the days when jewelry was important to me. I had grown up watching women who accessorized with jewelry. How important and brilliant were they to slide off those clip-ons, swinging the phone to their ears? Was Sian, with all of the attention focused on getting Magalee through her times tables, doing the equivalent?

I figured that Sian's need to decorate herself like a Bourbon Street Christmas tree was based upon her need to be noticed, to feel and be important. Didn't I spend the day feeling impor-tant? I had a staff of cooks who did just as I told them, and I was the object of considerable media attention as chef of a successful restaurant. Stepping into the dining room on a good night, when a menu change was being well received and an ar-ticle had just appeared, was thrilling—often I received a recep-tion worthy of Mick Jagger.

Though only five, maybe Sian was looking for the elation that came from the Mick Jagger reception. I knew no other way of providing this except through giving. And now, for the most part, all of my giving started in the kitchen.

So on Mondays, while Magalee was reciting her math facts, I played *sous*-chef to Sian as she made pasta. Pasta is so simple that a child can make it. And homemade pasta is so wonderfully tender and adaptable that it makes any day seem like a holiday. A few twists of the crank (the whole experience is reminiscent of the Play-Doh Fun Factory) turn the person wearing the apron into the evening's superhero.

BASIC PASTA

Winning hearts and minds in the kitchen and then the dining room is easy with a forty-five-dollar investment in a pasta machine. Many an early fascination with food begins with rolling pasta. Small hands can win raves in the dining room.

MAKES 6 FIRST-COURSE OR

3 MAIN-COURSE SERVINGS

3 CUPS FLOUR

1 TEASPOON SALT

4 EGGS, BEATEN

1 TABLESPOON EXTRA VIRGIN OLIVE OIL

1 TO 3 TABLESPOONS WATER

A SIMPLE SAUCE

⅓ CUP DICED SHALLOTS

16-OUNCE CAN PEELED PLUM TOMATOES, PULSED IN THE
BLENDER UNTIL ROUGHLY CHOPPED (ABOUT 5 OR 6 PULSES)

2 TABLESPOONS HEAVY CREAM

¼ CUP FRESHLY GRATED PARMESAN CHEESE

On a clean countertop with a good deal of space (or the dining room table) make a mountain out of the flour. Make a
well in the mountain large enough to hold the salt, eggs, and
oil. Using a fork and a circular motion, work the eggs and oil
into the flour. Continue to make circles with the fork to in-
corporate the wet ingredients into the flour. Add enough water to form a dough you can knead and work on the surface
without using flour to keep it from sticking. Knead the dough
quite a bit. Work more flour into it if necessary.

Follow the directions on your pasta machine (Imperia
makes a really good one and and it's affordable). You'll have
to cut the dough into 5 or 6 pieces and flatten each piece with
the heel of your hand. Then fold it over twice. Crank this
through the machine. Repeat this procedure 6 times. The
dough should be soft, but you should be able to manipulate it
without it cracking or tearing. If it is too soft and tears as
you roll it through your pasta machine, knead it with a little
more flour and start the folding process over again.

As you prepare to roll out the dough, keep some corn flour
or cornmeal handy. If the cut pasta begins to stick, toss a little
cornmeal over it before you hang it. Also, cover a dowel or
broomstick with plastic wrap. Prop the dowel across the top of
two open cabinet doors in the kitchen to hang the pasta on as

you're working with it. Start from the highest setting (6 on most machines) and crank the kneaded pasta through. Continue after lowering the setting to 5 and then all the way to the thinnest setting—1. You should have a smooth, long, thin sheet of pasta. Hang it on the dowel and let it dry until it no longer sticks to your fingers. Work on a few more pieces, checking the ones that are hanging. The pasta should be dry but not too dry or it'll break as you try to remove it from the dowel.

The pasta is ready to cut into linguini or spaghettini when you can squeeze the sheet between thumb and forefinger and it does not stick to your fingers. Fit the cutter attachment to your machine and cut the pasta into strips. Hang the pasta on the dowel and allow it to dry again. When you're halfway done, set 3 quarts of water, 1 teaspoon salt, and 1 teaspoon olive oil to boil in a large pot. While Sian cuts the pasta, I'm usually grating cheese, dicing shallots, and getting the sauce ready. The fresh pasta cooks in just under 2 minutes once tossed into the boiling water. You can use a strainer to carefully transfer it from the water to the pan, where your simmering diced shallots, tomatoes, and tablespoons of heavy cream await.

There are some variations to the pasta recipe that can bring "ooohs" and "aahhs." One of Sian's favorites is the "brocade," or what she calls "bedsheet" pasta.

BEDSHEET PASTA

*This is a sure way to bring drama to the dinner table.
It's easy to do but is one of those things that
turns a cook into an artist.*

MAKES 4 FIRST-COURSE SERVINGS

BASIC PASTA (SEE RECIPE PAGE 90)

2 TABLESPOONS FRESH CHERVIL LEAVES

2 TABLESPOONS FRESH TARRAGON LEAVES

1 TABLESPOON FRESH FLAT-LEAF PARSLEY LEAVES

12 STRINGS OF CHIVES

THE SAUCE

1 TEASPOON EXTRA VIRGIN OLIVE OIL

1 TEASPOON BUTTER

1/4 CUP FINELY DICED SHALLOTS

1/4 CUP MINCED CHIVES

1/2 CUP COARSELY CHOPPED WILD MUSHROOMS

1/2 CUP DRY WHITE WINE

SALT AND PEPPER

1/3 CUP GRATED PARMESAN CHEESE

*After you've squeezed the pasta through the thinnest setting,
instead of hanging it to dry, stretch it out on your cornmeal-
dusted table. Decorate the sheet of pasta with long strings of
chives and tiny fans of chervil, thyme, and tarragon leaves.
Just use leaves, no stems.*

Place another thin sheet of pasta over this one and carefully feed it through the machine again on the thinnest setting. The effect is like a botanically patterned fabric. Trim the edges of the brocade with a sharp knife before hanging it over the dowel. While your water is boiling, heat 1 teaspoon of olive oil with 1 teaspoon of butter in a skillet, add ¼ cup of finely diced shallots, ¼ cup of minced chives, and ½ cup coarsely chopped wild mushrooms (chanterelles are great for this recipe), and cook over medium heat for 2 to 3 minutes. Add the dry white wine. Simmer until reduced by half. Add a pinch of salt and a few shakes of freshly ground pepper.

After you've boiled the pasta for 2 minutes, carefully strain it and toss it in the pan of simmering mushrooms. To plate, carefully, with two wooden spoons, place a sheet of the brocade in the center of a salad plate. It should stand like a just dropped handkerchief.

Spoon the mushrooms and liquid from the sauce around the crowning drape of pasta. Sprinkle each with a little Parmesan. This makes a great first course. Guests are always exceedingly impressed and the "chef" is usually greeted from the kitchen with a round of applause. I've taught Sian to simply take her seat at the head of the table and nod graciously while spreading her napkin over her lap.

CARROT-SAGE SOUP

What led to the perfect fall soup is that I spent the day watching the clock. It was getting late and the soup

needed to be finished. The carrots weren't cooked
all the way, still sweet but soft enough to purée. Add
the sage for a soup that is uniquely carrot sweet and sage mellow.

MAKES ½ GALLON OF SOUP

2 LARGE ONIONS, COARSELY CHOPPED

2 TABLESPOONS VEGETABLE OIL

3 POUNDS CARROTS, PEELED AND ROUGHLY CHOPPED

½ CUP WHITE WINE

6 CUPS WATER

½ CUP HEAVY CREAM

4 BUNCHES (ABOUT ¼ POUND) FRESH SAGE, TIED WITH KITCHEN
TWINE

SALT AND PEPPER

In a large pot, sweat the onions in the vegetable oil. When
the onions are soft and translucent, add the carrots. Cook
the carrots and onions together, stirring constantly. Do not
let the carrots brown, but cook them until they glisten—
about 5 minutes. Add the white wine and simmer until it is
almost gone. Add the water and boil the mixture until you
can easily slide a sharp paring knife into the fattest piece of
carrot. Do not cook until the carrots fall apart. They should
be just tender. Purée this in a blender on the highest speed.
Return it to the pot and add the cream. Tie the sage to the
pot handle with the twine, using enough twine so that the
bunches are immersed in the pot. Let the soup simmer on
low heat for 20 minutes. Season it with salt and pepper to
taste. Discard the sage.

Five

EARNING EACH GRAY HAIR

The night I quit Evening Star was a Sunday. There was the usual After Brunch Beating, but this time, on my way home I got only as far as the pay phone at the gas station. I accepted an offer I'd received to run the big open kitchen at Breadline, a fast-paced bakery and lunch hall downtown, and I got back into my car and gave two weeks' notice to the owners at Evening Star. Still, I wondered if I'd done the right thing. I chain-smoked and sobbed as I drove home, feeling as if I had just given up my baby.

That night I dreamt a fitful dream of Nancy Sinatra, white boots, and the shiny wooden bar at the restaurant. I woke up so cold my teeth were chattering. It was a cool April night, but I had on two sweatshirts over my thermals.

Then I was hot. The sweatshirts came off and the thermal underwear was sticking to my back. My friend Jennifer came to check on me. I had managed to get on my chef pants, one boot, and a T-shirt—oops, I forgot the bra. Seeing my condition, Jennifer drove the girls to school. I succeeded in getting on the bra and had managed to get my head through the right hole in the T-shirt when the phone rang. I knew it was some-one from Evening Star, wondering where I was. I had never come in later than 9:00 without a phone call. Yes, it was 9:30. I was late for work. I apologized; I had given two weeks' notice but was on my way—I was not going to treat this lightly. "That's okay," they said, "don't bother. We'll manage. We ap-preciate all you've done and for ordering for us this morning. But we'll manage." Click. It was never really my baby. Maybe I was just the wet nurse who got a little carried away. And there they were gathering around her in her pastel yellow blankets, billing, cooing, tickling her round baby belly, and smearing lip-stick on her.

There was something toxic about working the way I was, so I got off the treadmill and succumbed to the virus. All that I had done to my body and spirit that year had caught up to me the night I finally let go.

I got back into bed. In a little over five delirious days, I emerged from a 106-degree fever in time to start my new job getting the kitchen ready to feed the hundred or so customers descending upon Breadline for lunch. It was five in the morning.

But things weren't right from the start. Saul, the night prep cook who came in at 4:00 P.M. and worked until midnight, wanted more money. Mark, the owner of Breadline, didn't like the ultimatum so he called Saul's bluff. I had only been there a week and Saul's work was piled on my desk. I was stumbling in at 4:00 just to keep up. The bakery needed twenty-five pounds of sautéed onions for the day's focaccia. There was never enough time to get the two cases of eggs boiled and peeled, and the five gallons of mayonnaise whipped up for the egg salad, and the lunch special and soup of the day made. I was chef at Breadline, but somehow I felt like just another prep cook with no say in who was hired and when. I was struggling to keep up with the daily chores with no time to manage staff, retool the recipes, or come up with new food to increase breakfast sales.

The best part about my day was that it was over by 5:00 P.M. I had the full day off on Saturday. Sunday I went to bed at 9:00 P.M. because my week started again at 4:00 A.M. Monday morning.

All day I cooked from someone else's confusing recipes and made Wednesday's soup even though all of the ingredients were out of season and five times what they cost in the winter or spring. Butternut squash in August is near impossible to get and when the farmer can harvest a full case of them they are the size of a banana. Still, Wednesday was butternut squash soup. I needed three cases of the tiny squash—now up to four dollars a pound. One Wednesday I lied and said the produce company couldn't get it. "They subbed yellow squash," I explained. I made a splendid summer squash soup with a spicy candied almond garnish. It sold out before lunch was over at a fraction of the food cost of the winter squash. But I could only pull these kinds of maneuvers when the boss was out of town. There was a wedding in California; this meant that I could ask the bakery to make a few dozen burger buns with some of the brioche dough. That and the surplus of ground turkey meant turkey burgers with a big ear of buttered white corn. Customers and staff hadn't seen anything like it. There was a giddy frenzy. I watched sophisticated suited Washington, DC, businesspeople making pigs of themselves crunching on corn on the cob. It was that old thrill coming over me again. I found myself pausing to take the time to watch customers devour the food I'd created.

But my boss complained that I was messing with the familiar. The customers had come to expect certain things on the menu and we were obligated to provide. The key to success here was consistency. Things weren't going great at work, but the hours gave me much-needed time to catch up on the mommy stuff. Although I was working downtown and had to battle meter maids, it was nice to have dinner with the girls every night.

I started to see what I had really been missing. I was able for the first time in years to pick them up from After Care. We could linger over dinner and sit at the big table in the dining room reading and doing homework. I got much more than my five hours on Sunday night. And that was a good thing. The day at Breadline felt like torture. I started my day in the dark and worked the hours approaching lunchtime as if there were a gun to my back. The hands on the clock whizzed around like fan blades until the doors opened at 7:00 A.M. When the lunch crowd streamed in, the clocked slowed like someone had cut the power. It seemed like hours passed before 12:30 clicked to 12:35. Finally, at 4:00 P.M. I was done for twelve hours. The girls would be coming home with me. They'd help me with dinner. We could be a normal family for a while and it was still daylight. But being a normal mother with normal children meant I had my hands full, discovering that not all of what I'd been missing was peaches and cream.

. . .

There have always been things about my children to worry about. My husband and I, living the American dream of working nine to five and paying a mortgage and a day-care center, hadn't had it all figured out. But there were two of us and the kids fit into a well-established routine.

When I started cooking for a living I had to figure out how to do this myself with no routine and a high-pressure job. It would have been great if when their father left town and I started cooking, the kids suddenly cooperated. But they didn't. There were mysterious headaches, falls, and the worst thing for the child of a chef, starvation.

Sian had been a robust baby. She was fat-cheeked and round, with a playful spirit that none of us were quite prepared for. Sian liked the dining room as her venue and put on a show at dinnertime regularly. She watched as we ate and spent most of her mealtime chatting. Or she'd rearrange her broccoli so it all faced north, and then wait for our reaction. She'd hold the chicken leg over the edge and let it fall. Her father, frustrated that his shouts and threats did not elicit the response he expected, would furiously leave the table. "Eat your dinner, Sian," he'd plead. Then, "Damn it, Sian, eat!"

Magalee was the peacemaker. Listening to her father get angrier and angrier with her younger sister sent her fork in motion. Sian would stop her giggling and just stare in wide-eyed disbelief. She was stunned by the fury she could create with a carrot slice or spoonful of rice. Stunned and intrigued. Not eating got so much more attention than eating. While her sister ate more, Sian ate less and less at every meal.

The habit continued long after her father was out of our lives. Sian weighed thirty-seven pounds at age four. But at her physical before first grade she weighed in at thirty-one. Lunch came back untouched. And no technique at dinner seemed to get her to eat. There were many nights of stomachaches and vomiting. The bones of her wrists and spine became more and more prominent and Sian began to get that sunken-eyed look of the starved.

The only thing that I could get Sian to eat with any regularity was saltines. There was considerable arm-twisting to get her to take a few bites of an apple. But a few days of crackers unfailingly led to a forced meal and then vomiting. There were few days of what Sian would later refer to in her journal as "stomach bliss," until I looked at what was coming out of her body as well as what was going into it.

I learned that the vomiting was probably caused by Sian being backed up. There was nowhere for food to go because the wall of crackers was blocking the exit. Sian was constipated. So crackers were eliminated and vitamins (they can increase the appetite) had to be introduced. I had put fruit in the meatloaf before to make sure some was in her diet. Now I set about changing my meatloaf recipe once again, and I created a meatloaf blended with prunes. It made for a rich gravy and smooth texture. It's a dinner to keep the whole family regular.

Not having her father around was showing on Magalee, who was struggling, too. She stopped paying attention in class. Her teachers related stories of her drifting off, staring out the window. Homework assignments gave her unbearable headaches. Tears and tantrums took up all of her homework time and it was late at night before the spelling sentences and math problems were completed.

I had to get Magalee through this bump in the road and get

her through elementary school all at the same time. Her disappearing acts in class and homework-induced headaches had her way behind the other students.

So I sat Mag down with an after-school bowl of stew, and worked to teach her all she missed in class. The small bowl of stew was enough to settle her down. It was grounding. It showed her it was safe to eat for no other reason than that she wanted to, that she was hungry or unsatisfied—it wasn't to please a parent but for her own personal health and satisfaction. Maybe I could beat back the headache of her missing father and help her think of herself and of school. I chose her favorite—a simple, slow-simmered beef stew—that I had started to make when practicing during cooking school. It had the benefit of being low in fat but high in protein and vitamins. If it made her eat less at dinnertime, that was fine, too. It was a much better snack than what many of her classmates were digging into after school.

I also thought it would help if Magalee got more physical activity. Now that I had a whole Saturday off, I thought it time I get her to learn to ride her Christmas present. But a couple of spills off her two-wheeler had her ready to give it up. No matter how much I encouraged her and how often I told her she was almost there and that I was ready to let go and let her pedal into the horizon without me holding on, she refused to get back on the flower-speckled banana seat.

It didn't take long before I was irritated and thinking that Magalee would never overcome her fears and would live in the attic of a suburban boardinghouse and never venture outdoors. "Fine!" I shouted. "Let's just leave it here on the sidewalk.

Maybe some other little girl will see it and want to ride it and take it home with her."

"That's a good idea, Mommy," she said, wiping her tears with her sleeve and nudging the kickstand down with her toe.

She marched up to her room while I settled on the couch with a newspaper. About a half hour later I heard her come down the stairs. I'm thinking, my plan has worked and Magalee will not be able to stand another girl riding off with her birthday present. "I made a sign, Mommy," she announced proudly. She showed me the brightly colored letters that read FREE BIKE FOR GIRL.

That little sign, that crayon-on-wide-rule resignation, had me off the sofa. I slapped that bike helmet back on her head and dragged her outside, telling her that she'd thank me later. When I let go and she pedaled to the end of the block, turned, and headed back to me with that smile that means independence, self-confidence, and fear be damned, I knew she was glad that no little girl had taken her bike.

Despite our challenges, I considered myself lucky. I had gotten pretty far in my child raising and hadn't once had a trip to the emergency room. Then the phone rang. When I picked it up and held the receiver to my ear, it sounded as if the Three Stooges were phoning in a sandwich order. I checked the caller ID. It was Sian's school's phone number. What on earth could have those normally cool, calm, and collected women in the main office suddenly upending file cabinets and tossing cups full of pens and pencils onto the floor?

My heart was pounding when I hit the redial. Mrs. Paul answered, her voice quivering. I imagined a few strands of hair had escaped from the hold of her normally well-centered bun.

"Mrs. Paul?"

"Yes?" the voice was hesitant, her usual main-office firmness gone.

"Did you just call me? This is Sian's mother."

"Yes, I know. I—" She was stammering. Now I was really scared.

"Is something wrong?"

"It's Sian. She, she hurt her arm." She chose her words carefully. I saw a picture in my head. Sian, lying in a pool of blood in the playground; her arm, completely detached, about three inches from its former home in her shoulder.

"Is it broken?" I managed.

"I don't know." She waited. She wanted me to say something. But I was busy imagining Sian and her arm in all of the ways she could have hurt it bad enough to call me and it's not broken—or is it? She finally gave in. "We've called an ambulance." I could hear the siren screaming through the receiver.

Sian's fractured ulna was the result of a slip from the monkey bars. She ran from the playground to the recess monitor with her now U-shaped forearm, not quite knowing what was wrong with it. I met the ambulance at Children's Hospital and about twelve hours later the arm was set and we went home. During the long wait, Sian confessed that her lunch had made her hands a little greasy and she hadn't been given the opportunity to wash after lunch. Her typical maneuvers on the monkey bars at school suddenly contained a new ele-ment of danger.

The culprit was a braised cube steak—great for dinner and the leftovers in a sandwich are irresistible, even to picky Sian, who will devour this sandwich, especially if it is made on a croissant. Be sure and pack a few paper towels and moist tow-elettes when you make this for lunch.

Sian chose the fluorescent pink cast. After it dried, the nurse advised me to give her Benadryl for the itch and plenty of calcium for the bones. I've never had trouble getting Sian to take medicine, but milk was an entirely different matter. And as I expected, Sian wanted Benadryl every hour and would have nothing to do with calcium unless it was hidden under the marshmallows in a scoop of rocky road.

A pink fluorescent cast can get you noticed. But after a couple of days and everyone has seen it, you're just somebody in a cast and nobody cares. You've got to keep the interest go-ing, I'm sure that's what Sian was thinking. And all of that thinking made that little arm itch like crazy. So the next week's challenge was to keep Sian from stumbling around in a Benadryl-induced stupor and re-breaking her arm, which was weak from a calcium deficiency.

I concocted a Benadryl placebo, plus gave her chocolate syrup, which tastes great in milk or over ice cream, and calcium-rich cannelloni. This placebo will replace any of that red liquid medicine your kid may be asking for too often. This can only be used, however, if you know your child. I can tell Sian has a fever without a thermometer. Her whole demeanor changes and pain is obvious in her face and posture. Just holding her on my lap or in my arms tells me when she is really suffering. On these occasions, I give her the real stuff as directed. But an itch is subjective and often is better relieved through the power of suggestion.

Sometimes you have to give in. I'm not sure if I learned that as a parent or as an employer. But both children and employees need to know that there might just be a prize involved. So there were the times that I went to an owner and lobbied for a fifty-cents-per-hour raise for a member of my staff. I did this quietly and without any fanfare. When it worked, the small reward silently appeared. His or her check was just larger. Not by much, but enough for them to notice. Someone had done a good job this week and I had noticed. Likewise with Sian, if I had gotten her to eat a whole pint of yogurt or have milk with her lunch, I would quietly squeeze a tablespoon or two of my homemade chocolate syrup in the bottom of a ten-ounce glass of milk. There'd be a big smile and for about three or four days there wouldn't be a heavy sigh when I placed a glass of the white stuff in front of her.

I think it was a lucent moment in Mrs. Schneider's seventh-grade science class when I actually sat up, rubbed my eyes, and wrote in my loose-leaf binder that spinach is also rich in calcium. But Mrs. Schneider did also insist that the liver had no function, so I took this spinach information with a grain of salt. I had to check this out.

Mrs. Schneider had been right about the spinach. Calcium and iron, just to name the short list. I was able to double up on calcium with cannelloni, one of the few things that was easy to get Sian to eat.

STOMACH BLISS MEATLOAF

GREAT FOR THE WHOLE FAMILY ONCE A WEEK

This recipe is one of those wonderful opportunities
to add a healthy ingredient that actually enhances flavor.
Over-ripe peaches or nectarines also add fiber and flavor.

MAKES A HEALTHY DINNER FOR 4

I LARGE ONION, DICED

I POUND GROUND BEEF (80/20)

3 EGGS

I TABLESPOON SALT

2 TEASPOONS PEPPER

½ CUP PITTED PRUNES, PLUS 5 OR 6 FOR GARNISH

⅓ CUP BREAD CRUMBS OR BROKEN OATS (CRUSHED BY HAND OR PULSED IN A BLENDER)

FLOUR FOR COATING MEATLOAF

½ CUP VEGETABLE OIL

I CUP WATER OR LOW-SODIUM CHICKEN STOCK

In a large bowl, work the onions into the beef with your hands until they are well distributed. In a blender combine the eggs, seasonings, and prunes. Blend until smooth. Add the prune mixture to the beef and work with your hands until thoroughly mixed. The more you knead the meat, the more tender and juicy your meatloaf will be, so work it well before adding the crumbs. Add the crumbs and work the meat mixture for about 10 more minutes. Shape into two small, elliptical loaves. Pat with the flour. In a large skillet, heat the oil over medium heat. Carefully place the loaves in the oil and brown on both sides. Turn them carefully, using two spatulas. After both are browned, remove them to a platter and pour off most of the oil. Add 5 or 6 prunes and cook over low heat. Add the water or stock, scraping the browned bits off the pan. Bring the liquid to a boil and then turn down to just simmering. Put the loaves back in the pan and cover. Let simmer over low heat for about 45 minutes to an hour.

POT-AU-FEU

IT IS BEST TO START PREPARING THIS DISH THE DAY BEFORE YOU PLAN TO SERVE IT. I WOULD BEGIN THE BOIL AT 3:00 OR 4:00 ON SUNDAY AND HAVE ENOUGH TO SERVE MAGALEE A 4-OUNCE BOWL EVERY DAY BEFORE WE STARTED HOMEWORK

This simmered away in a pot early one Saturday. A vegetarian friend was visiting and found the aroma irresistible. She stayed for dinner and ate meat for the first time in years.

MAKES 6 SERVINGS

3- OR 4-POUND BLADE CHUCK STEAK OR CHUCK ROAST (BONE-IN IS OKAY)

I ONION, QUARTERED

2 CARROTS, PEELED AND CUT INTO THIRDS

3 CELERY RIBS, CUT INTO THIRDS

2 SPRIGS THYME

SALT AND PEPPER

THE GARNISH

I CUP DICED NEW POTATOES

I CUP DICED CARROTS

I CUP PEELED WHITE PEARL ONIONS

Place the first four ingredients into a large pot and cover with 1 to 1½ gallons of cold water. Turn the heat to medium. When the liquid begins to bubble and the coagulants start to rise to the top, reduce the heat to low and skim off all of the fat and coagulants. You will need to continue skimming during the 6 hours you'll be simmering your stew, so stay nearby with a spoon. Do not let it boil. When the meat is tender, not falling apart into strings but really easy to chew, take it off the heat.

Strain the liquid and refrigerate it. You may need to use a fine strainer or coffee filter if you did not skim enough while it was cooking. Remove the meat to a cutting board and cut it into large cubes. Place the meat into a container and refrigerate overnight.

The fat in your stock will have risen to the top and hardened. You can discard this. Add the potatoes and carrots for the garnish, and bring your stock to a boil. Add the onions and boil until the onions are soft enough to be pierced easily with a toothpick. Reduce the heat and add the diced meat and thyme. Simmer for 3 or 4 more minutes, remove the thyme, and turn off the heat. Add salt and pepper to taste.

BRAISED CUBE STEAK

*I don't know what it is about this recipe, but like
so many that I've stolen from my mother it tastes
good, but never as good as hers.*

MAKES 6 SERVINGS

2 POUNDS CUBE STEAK, CUT INTO 5-OUNCE PIECES

SALT AND PEPPER

¼ CUP VEGETABLE OIL

FLOUR (ABOUT ½ CUP PLUS 1 TABLESPOON)

3 LARGE ONIONS, SLICED INTO THIN RINGS

2 CUPS LOW-SODIUM CHICKEN STOCK, OR WATER

Sprinkle both sides of each piece of steak with salt and pepper, while you heat the oil in a large, heavy-bottomed skillet. Coat each seasoned piece with flour. Over medium heat, brown each steak in the skillet. Cook for about 4 minutes per side, or until nicely browned.

Place the cooked steaks on a platter and set aside. Add the sliced onions to the fat and brown bits in the skillet and cook until wilted, about 3 minutes. Continue to cook the onions, scraping the caramelized bits of steak loose from the skillet bottom. Sprinkle the cooking onions with 1 tablespoon of flour. Stir constantly with a wooden spoon. The flour, onions, and fat should cook in the pan over low heat for about 4 minutes. Gradually add the chicken stock and continue to stir (constant stirring means you'll have no lumps of uncooked flour in the braising liquid—your gravy).

Increase the heat and bring this to a boil, then turn it to low again and add the steak to the onions and stock. Simmer on low heat for 45 minutes. The steak should be very tender. Remove it to a platter and season the gravy in the pan with salt and pepper to taste. This dish is great served with white rice. Leftovers make an excellent sandwich on a baguette or croissant.

PINK MEDICINE PLACEBO

Unfortunately it doesn't taste as awful as those things can taste. But it is sufficiently spiked to make Sian feel as if she's being medicated.

MAKES 5 OR 6 DOSES

1 TABLESPOON LEMON JUICE

4 TABLESPOONS CONFECTIONERS' SUGAR

1/4 CUP WATER

2 DROPS RED FOOD COLORING

1 DROP YELLOW FOOD COLORING

Combine all of the ingredients in a stainless-steel bowl. Whisk until the sugar is completely dissolved.

CHOCOLATE SYRUP

GREAT IN A GLASS OF COLD MILK OR WARM OVER ICE CREAM

When I first started, I used Hershey's cocoa powder
for this recipe. Valrhona's cocoa powder takes it
to a whole new level.

MAKE 1 ½ CUPS OF SYRUP

2 CUPS WATER

1¾ CUPS SUGAR

¾ CUP DUTCH-PROCESS COCOA POWDER

1 TEASPOON PURE VANILLA EXTRACT

PINCH OF SALT

In a nonreactive saucepan, whisk the ingredients together.
Over medium heat, stirring constantly, simmer the chocolate
until it thickens. It should coat a spoon. Cool and store in a
squeeze bottle.

SPINACH AND RICOTTA CANNELLONI

Fresh pasta and fresh spinach make this an irresistible first
course, or a light dinner if you start with a salad.

MAKES 3 FIRST-COURSE SERVINGS

16 OUNCES RICOTTA

4 CUPS SLICED SPINACH, STEMS REMOVED

2 TEASPOONS SALT

1/2 TEASPOON FRESHLY GROUND BLACK PEPPER

1/4 TEASPOON FRESHLY GRATED NUTMEG

6 SHEETS UNCOOKED BASIC PASTA (SEE RECIPE ON PG. 90), EACH
CUT INTO A 5-INCH SQUARE (YOU CAN STACK WITH WAX PAPER
AND CORN FLOUR IN BETWEEN, AND FREEZE THEM IN AN AIRTIGHT
PLASTIC CONTAINER)

Blend the ricotta, spinach, salt, pepper, and nutmeg in a stand mixer (such as a KitchenAid). Refrigerate for 30 minutes or so. Spoon 2 tablespoons of the ricotta-spinach mixture onto each square of pasta, about 1 inch south of the top. Roll the top in over the ricotta, and then continue rolling into a tight log. Gently place the cannelloni in a baking dish about 2 inches deep. You can place the rolls pretty close together. Pour in just enough water to cover the bottom of the baking dish to about a 1/8-inch depth. Place the cannelloni in the center of the oven at 400 degrees. It will take 20 minutes for the cannelloni to heat through. Take this time to make your sauce.

CRUSHED TOMATO SAUCE

This is the simple sauce that never fails me. If it's not tomato season, a can of whole plum tomatoes will do.

MAKES 4 CUPS OF SAUCE

2 POUNDS PLUM TOMATOES, CUT IN HALF AND ROASTED UNTIL
VERY SOFT

2 TABLESPOONS OLIVE OIL

1 RED ONION, DICED

2 CLOVES GARLIC, MINCED

1 SPRIG EACH OF FRESH OREGANO AND THYME

1/2 CUP PINOT GRIGIO WINE

SALT AND PEPPER TO TASTE

To roast the tomatoes, place them cut side down on a sheet lightly coated with olive oil. Set the pan in the center of a 375-degree oven. It will take 20 minutes for the tomatoes to soften and for the skins to loosen.

In a stainless-steel bowl, smash the tomatoes with a potato masher or a stiff whisk while the onions and garlic sweat over low heat in 2 tablespoons of olive oil. Add the herbs and seasonings. Add the wine and simmer until the wine is almost all cooked away. Add the crushed tomatoes and simmer for another 10 minutes or so.

By this time, the cannelloni should be ready to come out of the oven. The water should be almost all cooked away and the cannelloni good and hot. Spoon sauce to just cover the bottom of each dinner plate. Carefully, with a wide plastic or nonstick spatula, place 3 or 4 of the cannelloni on each plate. Spoon a little more sauce over the top and serve.

Six

CAREFUL WHAT YOU WISH FOR

I didn't last long at Breadline. As much as we tried, it just wasn't a good fit. I wanted different things for the kitchen, but this kitchen wasn't really mine. And maybe my boss didn't like sharing the food. Letting someone into the creative process can be difficult. There are people in any business who don't want help . . . who don't want anyone else's input no matter how much they ask for it. My first attempt to contribute to the breakfast menu—an egg in a nest (I used the bakery's great brioche and grilled it with clarified butter, delicately toasting it and poaching an egg in its center at the same time)—received raves. But it never made it onto the menu.

Before it was all over, I found myself training my replacement: a young bad-girl chef who had been at a restaurant in a funky part of town for years. I remembered meeting her years ago and scratching my head over her. She was wearing high heels, makeup, and a ring on every finger (the kind of physical adornment many of us kitchen wenches had long given up).

There was talk in kitchen locker rooms that she was recently unemployed. How she came to that end had us all gasping and shaking our heads as if the news were that someone we knew had finally snapped and had to be coaxed from a building ledge by the fire department. It turned out that she hadn't been very excited about doing a big catering job on her day off. The rumor was that she had served a selection of inedible canapés . . . octopus tentacles on burnt toast rounds . . . things like that.

She was introduced to me as a new addition to our staff on Monday. We'd lost a manager to the slicer when he cut his thumb on Friday (grilled Reuben day). I spent a week showing her what soups to make on which day, and how to make the falafel and grill the radicchio. By Friday she knew as much as I did. I knew what was coming Sunday afternoon when my boss called me to meet him on Monday at 9:00 A.M. at another restaurant. "Don't bother coming in to work at your usual time," he said. He put my paycheck for the week on the table. It wasn't in its usual envelope. It amounted to about half of my rent. I was done. I walked around the embassies off Connecticut Avenue. I had never been fired before. The writing had been on the wall, but that didn't make it sting any less.

The truth was, I had stopped trying to please my boss. I didn't think it was within my power any longer. As I passed the elaborate buildings and stonework I thought that when leaving Evening Star for the job at Breadline, I had jumped into the fire from the frying pan. The kids were at summer camp. At two hundred fifty dollars a week for both of them, I knew I had to be working to afford the next week. There didn't seem to be an end to the scratching and clawing for me.

But for the first time in months—perhaps because I hadn't

gotten up at three in the morning—I felt as if I was finally breathing. I could finally let go and stop trying to succeed at something when the deck had been stacked against me. As scared as I was, I felt as if a burden had been lifted. Now I could carefully choose my next step. Wasn't this part of the process of becoming a chef? There were going to be times when someone wasn't happy. It was a business of quick tempers and rash decisions. There were chefs being fired and chefs storming out of kitchens every day.

I dreaded telling my mother that I'd been fired, but I knew I needed her to take the kids for part of the summer while I went on interviews and cooked for prospective employers. "Is this really the career for a single mother?" she said. I braced myself for the "I told you so." As for the girls' father, I no longer had the nagging worry that he would use his parents' money and position to find me unfit and get custody. He bounced from one menial job to another and avoided paying child support. In fact, Hakim had pretty much disappeared. Visits were few and far between and he never wrote or called. I couldn't ask for his help. My attempts at making our divorce painless for the children had failed. He wasn't there for any of us. I was entirely alone as a parent and as head of the household. The big H on my tax return screamed that out loud.

A jobless single parent? Nothing felt more lonely, and the only way out was to get busy. I told everyone I knew in the business that I was back in the job market. It was much easier than sharing the news with my family. I helped out in a few kitchens to pay the bills and I called the headhunter that I'd met at the bar late one night at Evening Star. He was excited to hear from me.

Two months later we were hammering out the details before signing the contract. By July, I had again what I really wanted: a chef job at a restaurant getting ready to open. I also had the summer to help bring the building together and design my kitchen while having evenings—until opening day—with the girls to get them ready for the coming year at a new school. My new kitchen was in a place dubbed the Broad Street Grill, and it was created around the notion that a bar could have great food, show sports on big TVs, and still appeal to young families in an upscale northern Virginia neighborhood.

In October of 1998 the restaurant opened. The project had been almost a year in the making, with me coming on toward the end. But these owners had investors, years of experience, and about half a million dollars to spend on the project, and I was confident that I would be chef at this place for years to come. There was time and care in every detail. The hardwood bar was carved by Mennonite woodworkers in Pennsylvania. The sign and the sponge-painted ceiling trim were crafted by a famous local artist. An antique stained-glass window, rescued from a turn-of-the-century church that had been demolished, had been lent to the owners and became an eight-foot-high centerpiece in the dining room. The space was beautiful. And all I had to do was train the staff and produce the food that was going to make us all famous.

Thomas, one of the partners, assured me there was nothing to worry about. The bar was going to be the breadwinner. With alcohol budgeted to account for at least sixty percent of sales, the pressure was off me. I just had to give them something to make them thirsty. Matt, the other owner, insisted that the food had to be a draw. According to one of the many decent reviews, we were "raising the bar" by creating a casual neighborhood bar with really good food.

And the food delivered. It was as if my Evening Star fever had infected me as it had the sickly character in D. H. Lawrence's "The Rocking-Horse Winner." I had a Midas touch and felt I could do nothing wrong. That kitchen churned out flavored butters and roasted garlic aioli. There were shiitake-crusted lamb chops and russet-wrapped rockfish with radishes. That first crazy, busy week we were open I called out orders to the cooks in a voice tight with laryngitis. The cooks responded and we fell into a rhythm that made us feel invincible.

Unlike Evening Star and Breadline, busy at Broad Street Grill felt good. The week of training a seasoned crew was paying off. Skilled preparation was the key. All afternoon the elements of some pretty complicated plates were put together and lined up at the grill, sauté station, and salad station in one-quart plastic cups. I called the orders as tickets rolled off the printer. And when the finished plates came clattering under the heat lamp, I put on the finishing touches—a sprinkle of chopped chives, a tower of fried wonton strips, crisped slivers of shiitake mushrooms. Beautiful things were coming out of the ugliest room in the building. It was intoxicating. I was called out to the dining room dozens of times by people who couldn't believe sweetbreads could taste so good. They had to meet who was responsible.

There were many nights when we got "spanked." The long rope of tickets printing out in the kitchen draped down to the floor even after I'd just pulled another floor-length strip and stuffed it into the pocket of my chef coat. But while brisk food sales and a full dining room made Matt ecstatic, they did nothing for grumpy Thomas. On busy nights when Thomas was running food he would do what is taboo in just about every nice restaurant in America—he'd auction off the food. "Who had the steak?" he'd bark at a table of four, heavily engaged in conversation. He didn't wait for anyone to answer and just started tossing plates in front of whoever he thought should be having the steak. There were many nights when no one was sitting in front of that shiny varnished bar. Food sales took over and easily surpassed liquor sales, accounting for sixty-eight percent of the total.

We survived the Christmas slowdown and a short-staffed, open-all-day New Year's Eve. After that it seemed like overnight we were in the midst of one of the hottest Augusts in history. Most of my staff were on vacation, had been fired, or quit. Roshena, whom I had brought with me from Evening Star, was again rubbing management the wrong way and was fired on a night when I was out of town cooking at a wine dinner.

The long honeymoon was over. Suddenly things weren't going so well, and there were Friday nights with only four or five tables occupied. And in a meeting, Matt and Thomas had carefully constructed numbers showing that from opening day up to that point my food costs were on the rise—food costs had gone from twenty-nine percent to forty-one percent. I learned at the meeting that it was my fault that the staff couldn't cash their checks. It wasn't that the restaurant was being managed poorly or that deposits weren't being made. It was that spinach was being wasted.

I was feeling the pinch as much as my hardworking crew. Only I didn't have a second job to help pay the bills. My bank had returned almost every check I tried to deposit into my account. Broad Street Grill didn't have any money in the bank, and my paycheck wasn't worth the paper it was printed on. I was working, but still struggling to pay the rent and the babysitter. I was in trouble again.

Things weren't any easier at home. That fall there was a lice outbreak at the girls' school. I came home late and tired and kept them up brushing olive oil through their hair and hoping they'd be let back into the building in the morning. Once back in school, Magalee was still struggling. It seemed that the minute I got Sian to behave I was soon saying something like, "So let me get this straight, Magalee did what?"

There was a young student teacher left in charge of Magalee's fourth-grade class one morning. She was appropriately full of enthusiasm and bursting with new ideas. Nowadays young student teachers are instructed in all sorts of educational techniques that reach all types of different learners. We didn't have any of these different learners when I was in primary school. Everyone sat at their desk and got barked at just the same from Ms. Westbrook or Mrs. Hecht or Mr. Pfeiffer. Teachers today face all sorts of challenges with kids who have ADD (attention-deficit disorder) and ADHD (attention deficit/hyperactivity disorder). New approaches are invaluable.

Ms. Young Student Teacher had them form a big circle with their desks. This always brings noise and excitement. Hearts are racing with anticipation. "What could all this new and different classroom proximity be bringing us this morning?" I'm sure the fourth-graders were shouting to each other as they scraped their combination desk/chairs around the room. Ms. Y.S.T. got them all organized to form the circle that left a huge open space in the middle of the floor. Ms. Y.S.T. put a chair in the very center. The class was given a word and one lucky kid after another got to sit in that center chair and say the word and then tell Ms. Y.S.T. and the class what that word meant to them.

Well, on this crisp November morning, the kids' hair windblown from the gusts that swept the leaves about the playground as they waited to file into the building, Magalee was seated in that center chair. She bit her lip, waiting for Ms. Y.S.T. to hold her chin up high and announce this morning's word. Ms. Y.S.T. cleared her throat. The class held their breath. Magalee fixed her eyes on all of the faces around the room, then on Ms. Y.S.T.

The young student teacher was starting to smile as she read the word—first silently to herself. She was pleased with the word. She had chosen it last night. She had sat with her black daily planner (with so many blank pages), thinking, thinking. She would be alone with the class for an hour. She needed a good word. She sat and thought. She had a cup of herbal tea, and then thought some more. Then it came to her. Just the word. As if someone had whispered it in her ear. Just like that. Wow. What a great word. It would spark so much conversation—deep conversation. The children would learn all sorts of things about themselves, about each other, about the world. All from this one six-letter word.

She cleared her throat again. "The word today is," she said, her eyes fixed on Magalee, "father."

It started as an itch at the tip of her nose. But Magalee would never scratch her nose right there in the center of the classroom with twenty-nine kids staring at her. She bit her lip a little harder. The word rolled around in her head. It echoed like white noise and she couldn't hear the class whispering and then saying it aloud over and over again: father, father, father.

The itch went from the tip to inside her nose like a sneeze and then the vision in her left eye became blurry, then her right. She could feel the lines of wetness on her cheeks. Ms. Y.S.T. said it again. "Father." She presumed Magalee was thinking hard . . . maybe word associating. But it was just then that the spasm hit Magalee in the stomach like a blow. Her shoulders shot up, and then back down and the quiver jiggled her spine and made her shake in her chair a bit. Then her face was buried in her hands. The sobs came from her throat, deep and heavy, and with each muffled wail her body heaved and convulsed, folded in half in the little chair/desk in the center of the room.

Ms. Y.S.T. covered her mouth with her hand and stared. She pressed her fingers into her lips. It's just a word, she thought. The boys pointed their fingers, crouching in their chairs, and giggled and guffawed. The girls looked at each other and whispered, "What's going on?" It was the recurring nightmare of kids out of control—laughing, crying, and all the things she hadn't counted on without a thought on what to do about it. Could she slip out of the room and get help? Or flip wildly through the pages of her manual without them noticing? Mr. Brown, who could hear the commotion way back in the teachers' lounge, drained his cup of coffee and headed for his classroom.

Mr. Brown related the story to me without any attempt to mask his annoyance. He didn't want to know why or how the word pushed my daughter over the edge. Only that she had gone over the edge and it was a curious disruption that earned her an appointment with the school counselor, who found all to be fine. But Mr. Brown was more concerned about the assignments that hadn't been turned in, including the catalog of planets worth fifty percent of the term grade. It had been due the previous week and Magalee hadn't turned it in and hadn't offered any explanation as to why she hadn't done so. I talked him into giving me another packet of wire brads and construction paper and assured him that the project would be turned in by Friday.

Grateful to have another chance, Magalee retreated to her room with colored pencils, rulers, scissors, and glue. On Thursday morning she was all smiles and ready to finish up her catalog during library time.

Her behavior had the other kids in her class labeling her an oddball. For Magalee, friends this year were not so easy to come by. She had spent much of her time at aftercare reading or playing with her little sister until Sian was called away to join in a game with her circle of kindergartners. The playground was often a lonely place for Magalee.

But today one of those mysteries of the playground occurred and suddenly Magalee had two companions: a grubby-looking girl with braces and ill-fitting clothes and a big-eyed, undersize girl a bit on the clownish, goofy side.

"Mommy," Magalee said, waving at me, smiling the kind of big toothy smile I hadn't seen in a long while, "I've made friends." The wind was kicking up and scattering the leaves around us, pushing them across the pavement and up against the fence. She waved good-bye to her chums as we headed down the steps to the car. I was happy for her and relieved. This was another milestone crossed. Maybe she could get past feeling odd and ostracized, incomplete and disliked because she had no father in her life. "Did you finish your catalog?" I asked her and soon found it was just Sian walking with me in the twilight. Magalee had run back to the playground and seemed to be swirling around as wildly as the leaves that blew around her so hard and high that some were in her hair.

"My catalog!" She was panting, trying hard to breathe against the stiff wind. "I had it here with me. I was working on it here on this bench before those girls came over to talk to me." There was nothing on the bench except for a coat and a lunch box left behind. "Is that it over there?" Sian pointed to a piece of bright red construction paper, a ring of Saturn clinging to it. It was pasted to the fence with the brown and yellow leaves. "There's another piece over there." Sian was turned around now, pointing to a black page. The moon could not hold on and was under the leaves behind the swings.

Magalee ran to get the moon. It was a smudge of tiny sneaker prints. But that was all that could be salvaged. The wind had taken the rest into the woods surrounding the school. The catalog was gone. And it was twelve hours till Friday.

I preached about focus. I scolded and made predictions about not finishing school and living as a ward of the state. Magalee skipped dinner and wrote a report on the planets, working well into the night to finish a project Mr. Brown did not accept.

I determined that they needed to hear my voice in their heads to keep them from succumbing to their particular temptations. It was as simple as writing them a note in their lunch. I found that if I wrote on the skin of their banana they'd definitely read what I'd written them. Sometimes, just the lunch, made with great care and attention, showed them that I was thinking of them, and I theorized that it would make them think of me. Could I get the scolding and preaching to stay in their brains to be recalled just as they were about to commit petty larceny or toss a monkey wrench into their own futures? Maybe as they coughed melodramatically on their sandwiches to dispel any notion that they might share them, they would feel special and envied—pretty important qualities in the world of schoolroom status. They'd owe me. How could they let Mommy down now? I remembered how a fancy lunch made me feel special; would it work for my fatherless daughter, with a mother she didn't see enough? Magalee had a lot more to deal with than I did when I was her age, so I wrote notes on her banana and stayed up after work a little later at night to make her a fancy lunch. It starred one of her favorites. The chicken cutlet always made for a special lunchtime.

I won't always agree with their choices when they get older and decide that playing the viola just isn't what they want to do anymore or that cheerleading wins over ballet; I know I'll have to accept it. Having children can pull at your insides, because those little bundles of joy get too big to carry and start having minds of their own. Unlike their father, who had been in and mostly out of the girls' lives, I'd watched them grow and change and become their own people. I know there will come a time when I will really have to let go. I'm full of advice and guidance; as their mother I suppose I always will be. I can feel my influence waning. As it has with my "other children."

Everyone in this business knows that a good dishwasher is hard to find. It became a joke at Broad Street Grill when I was chef. The homemade lemonade was a simple but time-consuming recipe. Thirty lemons had to be thinly sliced and mashed with two quarts of sugar and five quarts of water. This became the dishwasher's job, in addition to keeping the pans clean and the plates in sanitized supply. No sooner had I taught a dishwasher the recipe and he had a couple of shifts to get really good at it than he would disappear—just stop showing up for work. It became known as "the Curse of the Lemonade."

But then there was Santos, the fourth dishwasher to learn to make lemonade at Broad Street Grill. He was a slight and quiet man from El Salvador who lived by himself above a liquor store three bus stops from the restaurant. The lemonade became his, as if it were his recipe. He made it effortlessly as soon as he came in at 9:00 in the morning. And at 9:15 he presented me my sample to taste in a tiny cream pitcher on a tray. I insisted he pour one for himself. "*Salud*," we'd pronounce together. Then, down the hatch. It was perfect every time. The tasting became a daily ritual for Santos. It was evident that he took pride in his lemonade. The kitchen staff referred to him as my son. I didn't mind the reference at all. And neither did Santos. He'd left his home years ago. Who knows how long it had been since he had seen his real mother. I was certainly a kind of surrogate. And I could never have asked for a more dutiful son. The lemonade was perfect every day and my kitchen was always clean. It was Santos who came to the rescue when there was a spill in the walk-in or who readied more seasoned flour for the onion rings when we were in the middle of a busy lunch.

It's not uncommon for kitchen staff and waitstaff to be referred to as "the family." Before the crowds arrive someone in the kitchen gets the job of searching the walk-in refrigerator for something to throw together to "feed the family." It's an opportunity for waitstaff and kitchen staff to bond, forge alliances, and lay the groundwork for recovery. There are tense moments on busy nights and mistakes are made on both sides of the line. The staff needs to be able to move on and let go in order to recover and work together the following night no matter how much shouting and name-calling went on the previous night.

Kitchens are all different—chef standards, procedures, recipes, and where things go make up a considerable learning curve. A new cook or dishwasher can spend weeks just figuring out where things go and how to do things. Years before I had a kitchen of my own, I'd been given many opportunities to "parent." When I was a senior line cook at Cashion's, Chef would say in a voice quickly losing patience, "Would you show your son where the clean spatulas go?" But after he'd been there a month, he used the downtime on a slow night to scrub the carbon buildup off the entire rack of sauté pans. That's when I'd start soaking chicken in buttermilk for "my son's" fried chicken dinner.

Young cooks often become the charges of the more experienced staff. I've raised a few successful "children" as *sous*-chef and chef. There are the ones who have made me proud and gone on to do fabulous things—become successful food writers, cookbook collaborators, cooks in Australia, *sous*-chefs—and like most parents, I have children who didn't live up to what I thought was their potential. Cooking with brilliance and ease was just one of those things that they did, but it wasn't as interesting to them as computers. Or they moved in with the wrong guy. Or they couldn't stop drinking. I hear from my "children" every once in a while. We have the memories of combat veterans. With a phone call or postcard they remind me of the stress and hard work that bound us together and how during every busy night we'd pull together and make it through. Successful up-and-coming food-service professional or unemployed great cook living in subsidized housing—they are all my children.

BREADED CHICKEN CUTLET ON A KAISER

*You can use chicken breast. But I think thigh meat
has more flavor. Either way, they'll know
you care when you make this for lunch.*

MAKES 6 SANDWICHES

6 SKINLESS, BONELESS CHICKEN THIGHS

SALT AND PEPPER

3 EGGS

I SMALL ONION, CHOPPED

I TABLESPOON DIJON MUSTARD

I CUP FLOUR

I CUP BREAD CRUMBS

½ CUP VEGETABLE OIL

I TEASPOON BUTTER

6 KAISER ROLLS

6 LEAVES BOSTON LETTUCE

Cut each thigh in half. Cover each piece with a sheet or two of wax paper and pound it with a meat mallet until flat and round and about ⅛ inch thick. Sprinkle each piece with salt and pepper and set aside. In a blender combine the eggs, onion, mustard, a pinch of pepper, and 2 pinches of salt. Blend until totally smooth. Pour the egg mixture, the flour, and the bread crumbs in separate large bowls.

Coat each piece of chicken with flour. Shake off the excess. Dip it in the egg mixture until coated and dripping. Let most of the excess drip off and then coat completely in bread crumbs. Do this with all of the chicken pieces and set aside.

In a large sauté pan, heat the oil and butter over medium heat. When the butter sizzles and starts to brown, add 3 pieces of the chicken. Do not crowd the pan. Cook for 5 to 6 minutes per side and then drain on paper towels. Repeat with the rest of the chicken. Split a kaiser roll and butter both top and bottom very lightly. Place a leaf of Boston lettuce on the bottom and put the chicken on top of that. A slice of tomato or a few thin slices of cucumber on the chicken, under the top of the bun, work well, too.

THE CURSED LEMONADE

It packs a powerful punch and is so tart you can feel it in your tonsils. Some of our customers tone it down with a little extra ice.

MAKES ALMOST 1 GALLON

1 QUART SUGAR

15 LEMONS, WASHED WELL AND THINLY SLICED, ENDS DISCARDED

2 QUARTS WATER

2 QUARTS ICE

Mash the sugar into the lemon slices with a heavy wire whisk or wooden spoon until the fruit and the rind is pulverized and the sugar is dissolved. Stir in the water and ice. Stir this until well combined. Strain through a fine sieve.

FRIED CHICKEN

The buttermilk soaking is the key.
The buttermilk tenderizes and the garlic adds flavor.

MAKES 4 SERVINGS

ONE 3-POUND CHICKEN, CUT INTO 8 PIECES

1 QUART BUTTERMILK

6 CLOVES GARLIC, CRUSHED

1/3 CUP TABASCO SAUCE

4 CUPS FLOUR

4 TABLESPOONS SALT (PREFERABLY SEA SALT OR KOSHER)

1 TABLESPOON FINELY GROUND BLACK PEPPER

2 CUPS VEGETABLE OIL

1/2 CUP BUTTER

Soak the chicken in the buttermilk with the garlic and Tabasco for at least 2 hours. Sift together the flour, salt, and pepper. Heat the oil and butter over medium heat until the foaming of the butter starts to subside. Pull the pieces of chicken out of the buttermilk one at a time and coat well in the seasoned flour. Shake off the excess and place the chicken in the bubbling oil. Cook 10 to 12 minutes on each side. The juices should run clear when you pierce the thigh or leg with a fork. A good way to tell that the chicken is done is to watch the bones. When blood is bubbling out of the ends of the chicken bones the piece of chicken is nearly done. Continue cooking for 2 more minutes.

Seven

CRAVING A COMFORTABLE SPACE

My time at Broad Street Grill came to an end. We were growing apart. Matt and I started the project knowing where we wanted to go. But when he came back from vacation and the restaurant was even further in the red, he lost faith. I still believed. But I was the only one. Thomas had always been an outsider. He knew we needed to serve food, but the bar was what made his eyes twinkle. He smirked at the lamb chops and suggested effort be put into spicy wings and things like that. During that hot, slow summer he lobbied for the kitchen to be made over into an easy moneymaker. "We could just make this a pizza parlor," he said, looking at the labor figures. "We wouldn't need a chef or all of this staff."

I felt as if the world were scheming against me and I trusted no one before I handed in my resignation—green crayon on a bar napkin. A salesman from a strange meat supplier was sitting at the bar with Matt and Thomas. Jalapeño poppers, boxes of kid-size hot dogs, and other processed foods were mysteriously filling the freezer. They had hired an alcoholic ex–Red Lobster manager to "help me out" in the kitchen. He'd leave the kitchen through the swinging doors that led to the bar after the Saturday fray was over and knock back straight bourbon. By the time I'd checked the walk-in cooler and ordered for the next day he'd have drained four shot glasses and the bartender would be pouring him another. "See ya tomorrow, Shhheff," he'd cry out to me with a wink and a raised glass, the amber liquid sloshing over its boundaries.

I winked back, confident that I was on my way to a new job and maybe a James Beard Award nomination. I had already started creating the menu in my head—herb-grilled lamb chops, seared breast of duck, stewed rabbit, foie gras. In just a few days money would be no object. I could cross that threshold—menu items beyond the twenty-dollar restriction. Woo hoo. Now the whole town could take notice—get a load of me. In a few days I was going to enter a new kitchen as chef. This kitchen fed the who's who of Washington, and I could hardly contain myself. I planned wine pairings and researched exotic ingredients. I told all of my industry friends to look for me somewhere fabulous, but withheld the name of the place. I waited for the night of my debut to formally announce that I'd finally landed the job I was born to do, leading a landmark restaurant into a comeback.

When I handed Matt that napkin with the green crayon I was no longer part of Broad Street Grill. There were whispered and hushed conversations all around me. I was spoiling the fun. I was standing in the way. I'd given two weeks' notice but it was unbearable. One morning I just stopped coming. They didn't need me. Shoot, they didn't even want me around. That night a sob-choked staff called me at home. One by one in bro-ken English, in Spanish, in Korean—even in Ebonics— they asked why and begged me to come back. The ex–Red Lobster drunk was wearing all white—white shoes, white pants, white chef coat—like a wolf in sheep's clothing. To the staff that of-ten saw me working beside them in a black T-shirt with my apron stained with beef blood, that all-white outfit was a dec-laration that this new chef wasn't going to get dirty. Who was he? Wasn't he just another cook? The tickets were going wild that night. The printer was spitting them out like in the old days. My shoes were suddenly a little too big and tempers were flaring. I could hear angry voices and the rushing around of a busy kitchen coming through the phone. Mr. Red Lobster shouted, "Get out of my kitchen!" to one of the servers.

Roshena was working in downtown DC passing out flyers for a hair salon. She had no idea that I'd left Broad Street Grill. She had cashed her check and taken the train to come visit me. They told her I wasn't there anymore. She shook her head and told the bartender that Thomas and Matt had "fucked up a wet dream." They should have left it alone, she said. "Why when things are going good they gotta mess it all up?" She ordered a beer anyway in my honor and finished it alone at that polished hardwood bar. "Why, why, why, why?" she asked almost seriously, before she gave in to her trademark witch's cackle.

I had some misgivings about leaving Broad Street Grill for my new kitchen at Mrs. Simpson's. Here I was, leaving another place that I'd built, another baby I was leaving for greener pas-tures. Maybe I would never have left if there hadn't been sud-denly no more room for me at the table. But the millionaire who bought Mrs. Simpson's had lofty and generous ideas of putting the landmark establishment back on the map. He had me convinced that together we would be building something the likes of which the city had never seen.

There was talk that the dusty old place named for the Duchess of Windsor had just faded away and not kept up with the food movement sweeping Washington, DC. They had tried everything to keep up but the anchor had already been tossed into the water. I found tattered recipes for quesadillas and spring rolls, kind of lowbrow for the likes of Wallis Simpson. Flyers that were to be handed out at bus stops advertising the death knell—happy hour—were piled all over the office. I had heard rumors that bankers and attorneys had taken over; frivolous spending and personal problems had cost the owning family its decades-long ownership, and all the new owner had to do was pay off the creditors.

Mr. Bloomer dreamed of bringing back the Mrs. Simpson's of his memory. He had been a regular customer. So had Katharine Graham, Tip O'Neill, and a bunch of other heavyweights. When he and his wife came to Broad Street Grill on the recommendation of a friend that I might be the one to rescue Mrs. Simpson's from oblivion, they had the salmon tartare and the garlic-crusted halibut with salsa verde.

"This food," said Bloomer, using a jagged piece of torn ciabatta to sop up the green on his plate. "This is just what I'm talking about. You're wasted out here in this place, in this town." He outlined the room with his outstretched arms and then the entire city of Falls Church.

Mrs. Bloomer patted my hand and invited me to join them at Mrs. Simpson's for dinner that Friday. "See the place for yourself," she said. "It will help you come to a decision." I'd already decided. There was nothing I'd rather do than be chef at a place I'd admired before I'd even started cooking for a living. I'd noticed the magazine ads when I'd first moved to DC. The tiny notice in the upper-income-targeted magazine was simply stated: just that black-and-white photograph of Edward in that gray suit gazing lovingly at his bride, Wallis. She looked out into the distance. Her broad hat partly obscured her face, but if you looked closely you could see that slightest upturn of her lips. "I win," those thin, gray lips were saying. Edward was giving up the throne for this woman. All I had to do was give up on the Broad Street Grill. Like Edward I, too, was doing it for love. I loved the idea of being the chef of Mrs. Simpson's. Wasn't that what I'd been striving for since I got on this track? Finally, I would be cooking in a restaurant with deep pockets and wealthy customers. Isn't that what all of us dreamed of? I was peeling off the shackles of "How much is that special?" and the collar of "What comes with that?" Money was no object to the Mrs. Simpson's clientele. They had the income and sophistication to appreciate the menu I was planning. And it's foie gras that gets the attention of the James Beard House, I thought, not meatloaf.

Like many of the old clientele that once glided across the mosaic tile floors at Mrs. Simpson's, the restaurant was showing its age. It definitely lacked the polish of the new places that were dominating the District's dining scene. But the old photographs of the divorcée and her royal second husband, along with the museum-like memorabilia, added to the charm of the place. I had on my rose-colored glasses. Maybe Edward and I were the only ones who thought Mrs. Simpson was beautiful.

They'd hired a chef to reopen the place, and aside from this guy, who wasn't working out, all the grand opening had cost the millionaire was a nineteen-dollar banner that read UNDER NEW MANAGEMENT. Here was a chef who was lying to a full dining room. When I visited, the béarnaise sauce on my steak was mayonnaise spiked with tarragon vinegar, dried parsley, and an egg yolk. The mashed potatoes were instant with skins. I smiled to myself, pushing the food around on my plate. It was inedible. Looking around the dining room I could see the famous Washington faces smiling, enjoying themselves. My food would push them over the top. Surely they'd be slapping each other when *my* seared tenderloin with béarnaise sauce crossed their lips.

I accepted the job without hesitation. We talked about my start date, VIP dinners, upcoming holidays, and staff (Mr. Bloomer had found Maria, the old kitchen manager, to help me "bring back the old flavors"). He was a self-made man, he told me. We had a lot in common. He worked hard for his money and didn't spend it frivolously. He dressed well, but not in custom-made shirts or suits—the ones off the rack were just fine. "And he's fair," Mrs. Bloomer said, looking at me seriously. "So fair that he sleeps like a baby at night."

As a kid he delivered bread for his father's bakery. There was no time for a formal education. What he learned on the streets of his working-class neighborhood was schooling enough. Then there was his apprenticeship in trading. There were things one didn't learn in school. I shifted a little in my seat. I grew up with a different set of values. My family was built on formal education. My mother was the first in her family to go to college, and she received a full scholarship. She started a tradition that led to all five of her children enrolling. Months after completing the requirements for my degree, I taught English at a prestigious DC high school. But I never used my larger vocabulary as a weapon. And surely I appreciated and accepted the volumes of street knowledge to be had.

Although we took different paths, we'd wound up on the same square. There was no doubt that Bloomer was successful. He had the drive and determination to get by without that piece of paper. I respected that and found him charming and interesting. There was something to like about a guy who saw black and red so acutely, but still understood what a fine restaurant meant to people. Even if the numbers didn't all add up right away—and maybe it took a little while before the restaurant showed a profit—some things are bigger than money. I always felt that sometimes we can let our emotions take over, within reason; things don't have to be held together by the logic of plus and minus. Mr. Bloomer, probably pushing seventy, had a full head of hair with a reddish peroxide glow that masked the gray. Here was a man who understood the value of transcending reality.

"We have plans for the back room," Mr. Bloomer said, smiling. The purchase of the restaurant was a pricey interruption of a plan that was already in place. The Bloomers were building their art collection. Many of these priceless works were to decorate the private party room at Mrs. Simpson's. The photographs, medals, gloves, handkerchiefs, books, and other things that had belonged to Wallis and Edward would be taken down. The new room would be a gallery of fine art.

I was led to the back room, where the first painting, leaning against a low easel, came close to touching the ceiling. It was a nude with a long neck and broad hips. She stood in front of layers of blue drapes—teal, aqua, navy, turquoise. "You know what is so fabulous about this painting?" I had had a glass of wine with dinner and maybe that was affecting my perception of the quality of this work. I could see nothing fabulous. Mr. Bloomer was beaming, his chest swelling like a proud pigeon's. I could tell he wanted me to see what he was seeing. He was smiling and stood so straight that his heels left the floor and he was standing on his toes. I'm certain if he had known me better he'd have jumped up and down. He tugged at my sleeve, urging me to stand where he was standing; that way I could see the painting through his eyes. "Go on, go on," he was rooting for me. "Can you see it?" I was trying. I didn't want to disappoint him. I stood where he wanted me to stand, blinked my eyes, adjusted my glasses, and concentrated. "Can't you see it, what is so fabulous and unusual?" He waved his hands in front of the painting. I could tell he was getting frustrated with me. I humbly gave in and the answer burst from his lips as if he couldn't hold it any longer: "It's, it's . . . the pubic hair." And yes, there it was: a wispy dark triangle of black. There was more of that than there was hair on her tiny head.

I had another glass of wine at the table. I tried not to think about the décor. Maybe no one would ever see that room. I had to focus on the food. I held on to the notion that there would never be enough pubic hair nudes to hang. After all, Mrs. Bloomer was still undecided about the paper towels for the ladies' room. Plus, she had her hands full at home.

I was comfortable in my third week as chef of Mrs. Simpson's. It felt right. It felt like mine. There was even a sign at a parking space in back that read RESERVED FOR THE CHEF OF MRS. SIMPSON's. I pulled into my parking space and brought my 1981 Volvo to a halt as Mrs. Bloomer pulled in beside me in a smaller black Mercedes than I'd seen her in before. I was glad it hadn't rained that morning. The cable that flipped my wipers had snapped. I was hoping to be able to get that fixed in a couple of paychecks. Mrs. Bloomer's car chirped as her doors locked. When I asked her how she was, she looked down and shook her head. "It's a C-class," she said. "Mr. Bloomer is going to be very upset that the service department couldn't give us an S-class loaner car."

Despite our differences, I wanted more than anything to make this work. I wanted to settle down and be Chef somewhere for the long haul—to exercise partnership and profit-sharing options. I also worried that my changing employment status would be a source of anxiety for the girls. I watched for changes in their sleep and eating habits. What did their teachers think? Were they making friends? How did I wind up being the most unstable thing in their lives? I wanted nothing more than to be predictable. Things could be a little less interesting. That would be fine. Heart-pounding uncertainty could derail my single parenting. I was prepared to build a nest in the chef's office at Mrs. Simpson's or chain my ankle to the old Montague stove.

And each new restaurant and each new monogram on my chef coat was like starting over. I had to learn to operate new equipment, build an appropriate menu, get results out of my staff, work my way around a new boss, and organize the bull pen of babysitters to fit a new schedule. Never in my wildest dreams, whether in high school imagining my future, planning my life, or choosing a college, did I think that I would be a single mother of two. I had not prepared for this lifestyle. I was learning as I went along.

There were those days when the girls spent their evenings in my office, Sian studying for a spelling test or Magalee writing her *Island of the Blue Dolphins* book report on my computer. All I really wanted was for them to grow up as I did. My parents weren't perfect. But there are a couple of things they did with us, rituals that shaped me and that I'll never forget. Eating around that big table—all seven of us every night without fail, unless someone had a game or was in the school play—was one of them. I've moved three hundred miles away, but the siblings who still live in New York often can't resist my father's cooking and the familiar talk and humor of that table. Sunday brunch is pretty well attended.

My best attempts at replicating all of this had to be done while I helped Magalee with her homework; she had not developed any study habits and was still struggling. Yet my quick dinner preparation still had to provide me time to spend a minute or two reading to Sian. I had so little time that dinner had to be easy, and it always had to be something Sian would eat. So often I turned to one-pot roasted chicken with potatoes.

For a single mother in the restaurant business, birthdays can be a great source of anxiety. Often, my girls' special days fell when I had to be at work. This meant their celebrations had to happen on alternative days. I guess the guilt of not being like their friends' mothers—I worked weekends and nights and met with their teachers smelling of food and wearing chef pants and big boots—made me want to make the day an event. This was the day I made their favorite dinner, the dessert of their choice, and invited all the people we knew. Magalee's birthday favorite: cornflake-coated pork chops. Sian's birthday favorite: potato-crusted Dover sole.

With the promise of great food, the birthdays were always well attended, and happy, well-fed guests lavished plenty of attention upon the honorees. The girls never minded the postponed birthdays.

A chef's household is no different in many respects from that of the average American. Dessert has always been a popular meal in our house. Young Magalee would put her fork down, and with a pale green pile of lima beans still on her plate, she'd announce, "I'm full, Mommy. What's for dessert?" When I'd explain that if she was too full to eat her vegetables she'd have to be too full for dessert, she'd respond thoughtfully, "Oh, no, I've got a separate pouch for dessert," pressing her finger into that empty part of her stomach.

Ours was not a house where things were done and rules obeyed under threat of punishment. The girls and I negotiated and made bargains. There were no spankings. Instead there were nights when computer and TV screens remained dark, invitations were declined, and pleasures were withheld—dessert being the most immediate and accessible privilege always ready to be revoked. The parent who punishes by refusing to open that new gallon of ice cream also enjoys the added benefit of a discipline tool in which the rest of the family can participate and make sting even more.

Being one of five children who had to watch as my siblings enjoyed a bowl of mint chocolate chip, I understood the complex interplay of taunting, false pride, prolonged ice cream eating, and exaggerated enjoyment that compounds the punishment. I was never sent to bed without dinner. My father considered that a necessity. But the late-night sweet was a luxury. Eliminating the luxury of TV or dessert can turn a Cape Cod into a federal prison.

In order for this form of discipline to be effective, a routine must be established. Withholding dessert from the misbehaving child is most effective when the children in the household come to expect dessert over the years. It becomes more than just a privilege, it's a right. However, your charges must understand that rights can be taken away. A prisoner in a penitentiary has the right to twenty-five minutes of outdoor exercise daily. Yet, one misstep can mean undetermined days of solitary confinement.

Discipline, especially with young children, works best when it follows a simple formula: $A + B = C$ (good behavior + finish your dinner = dessert in our house). It's amazing how good everyone is if they've paid attention in the supermarket and watched me pick up that mint chocolate chip that was on sale. Or if there is a substantial amount of leftover birthday cake in the refrigerator.

Consistency is key here. Not just in administering the repercussion, but also in addressing the everyday. Dessert every night after dinner, however, takes planning, creativity, and, sometimes, a few simple recipes.

The stash of ice cream, frozen fruit bars, and the like in the freezer are fine staples. But dessert can also be a great way to introduce fruit into their diet when the season allows. When they were really young, I could pass off a bunch of red seedless grapes as dessert. These soon lost their luster, though, after making frequent appearances in the lunch box. I still rely on apples tossed in sizzling butter with a pinch of cinnamon and sugar as a healthy dessert alternative. In the summer, a tablespoon of sugar tossed over a pound of washed and halved strawberries right before dinner also scored high with Magalee. However Sian, who was not a big fan of strawberries, didn't mind missing this one and was tempted to skip her green beans when she saw the bowl of macerating berries on the kitchen counter.

The freezer is somehow looked on as the treasure chest in the minds of young dessert lovers. When I strained this strawberry concoction, added the strained juice of a freshly cut watermelon, and partially froze this psychedelic red liquid in a shallow baking pan, not even young Sian could resist the fruity-sweet icy shards piled into a bowl and set before her. She'd even eat the tiny cubes of melon and berry garnish hidden under the whipped cream.

ONE-POT ROASTED CHICKEN
WITH POTATOES

A delicious time-saver that you can dress down for a midweek meal, but also suitable for those times when company comes.

MAKES 4 SERVINGS

ONE 3-POUND CHICKEN (FRESH IF YOU CAN GET ONE)

2 CLOVES GARLIC, CRUSHED

I TABLESPOON SALT

I TEASPOON FRESHLY GROUND BLACK PEPPER

I TABLESPOON OLIVE OIL

8 TO IO SMALL NEW POTATOES, SCRUBBED AND CUT IN HALF

I ONION, QUARTERED (IT'S FOR ME—THE GIRLS WON'T EAT IT; SO ADD MORE IF YOU LIKE)

2 SPRIGS FRESH THYME

2 TEASPOONS FLOUR

I CUP LOW-SODIUM CHICKEN STOCK, OR WATER

Preheat the oven to 450 degrees. Rinse the chicken inside and out, and pat dry with a paper towel. Fill the cavity with the garlic, and some salt and pepper. Place the chicken in a baking pan just large enough to hold the chicken with about an inch or two to spare on the perimeter. Rub the bird with the olive oil, tuck the wings under, and tie the legs together loosely just to cross at the ankles. Sprinkle the oiled skin with salt and pepper. Place in the center of the hot oven.

When you hear the sizzling and popping ("singing" as it's called) and the bird is beginning to brown, reduce the heat to 350 degrees. Add the potatoes and onions around the bird. Roast for an additional 45 minutes or so. Cooking time should be 20 minutes per pound. Prick the thigh and the juices should run clear.

Transfer the chicken to a warm platter and surround it with the potatoes and onions (you could leave them in the pan and brown them a little more on the stove top if you like, then remove them with a slotted spoon). Pour most of the fat out of the pan but for a tablespoon. Toss the thyme and flour in the pan and turn the heat to medium. Scrape the bits of baked-on chicken and cook, stirring, for about 2 more minutes. Pour in the chicken stock or water. Simmer for 5 minutes or so. Remove the thyme and pour into a gravy boat.

CINNAMON APPLES

A little butter, a little sugar, and a little cinnamon turn apples into dessert. Keep a blend of cinnamon-sugar in an airtight container in the spice cabinet. I've always found that ready supply sparks creativity.

MAKES ABOUT 4 DESSERT SERVINGS

6 BRUISE-FREE TART APPLES (GRANNY SMITH OR MCINTOSH)

2 TEASPOONS BUTTER

3 TABLESPOONS SUGAR

I TEASPOON GROUND CINNAMON

Peel, core, and slice the apples into eighths. Melt the butter over low heat in a medium-size sauté or frying pan. Stir in the sugar and cinnamon. Add the apples and toss or stir until coated with the sugar and butter. Continue to simmer over low heat until the apples are starting to soften, 3 to 5 minutes. Serve warm.

STRAWBERRY-WATERMELON GRANITA

Cranberry juice and apple juice also make great
frozen dessert. Add a splash of pineapple juice and
it is still fat free and good for you.

MAKES ABOUT 4 DESSERT SERVINGS

2 PINTS STRAWBERRIES

1/2 CUP SUGAR

6 CUPS CUBED AND SEEDED WATERMELON

2 CUPS WHIPPED CREAM

Wash, trim, and halve the berries. Toss with the sugar in a nonreactive bowl. Set aside for 1 hour (the sugar will dissolve into the berries and draw out the sweetened strawberry juice).

Blend the cubes of melon in a blender on a high setting (liquefy or purée). Strain the liquid from the pulp (you can also press the pulp with a spoon to extract the liquid). Then strain the juice from the berries. Combine the juices (you should have about 4 cups of liquid) and pour into a shallow baking dish. Discard the berries. Freeze for 45 minutes, or until just starting to ice over. Remove from the freezer and with a spoon or fork, stir and break the shards of ice. Freeze again for another 20 minutes and then remove, repeating the breaking and flaking of ice. Freeze again and repeat, breaking and flaking the ice until there is no more unfrozen or unflaked juice. Spoon into chilled bowls and garnish with whipped cream.

MAGALEE'S FAVORITE CORNFLAKE-COATED PORK CHOPS

*I first noticed the recipe for cornflake-coated chicken
on the cereal box. It's easily translated to pork chops.
I prefer the flakes broken gently in a blender
rather than the already processed crumbs.*

MAKES 6 SERVINGS

1/4 CUP UNSALTED BUTTER

2 TEASPOONS SALT, PLUS 1/2 TEASPOON

1 TEASPOON FRESHLY GROUND BLACK PEPPER, PLUS 1/4 TEASPOON

3 EGGS, WELL BEATEN

1/2 CUP FLOUR

4 CUPS CORNFLAKES, COARSELY GROUND IN A BLENDER WITH
1 TEASPOON SALT

6 CENTER-CUT RIB PORK CHOPS (ABOUT 10 OUNCES EACH,
1 1/2 INCHES THICK)

*Preheat the oven to 400 degrees. In a deep, heavy baking
dish, melt the butter in the oven. Add 1/2 teaspoon salt and
1/4 teaspoon pepper to the beaten eggs. Sift the remaining salt
and pepper with the flour into another bowl. Place the flour,
eggs, and cornflakes in large separate bowls. Coat each chop
with flour, dusting off the excess. Then coat in the egg. Toss
the chops into the cornflakes, flip, shake, and completely
coat with the crumbs. Set each chop in the baking dish and
then turn so that the top and bottom of each chop is covered
with butter. Place in the hot oven for 20 minutes. Then,*

with a fork, turn each chop and finish baking the chops for another 20 minutes on the other side.

SIAN'S FAVORITE POTATO-CRUSTED DOVER SOLE

*Potato crusting is great on rockfish and grouper as well.
Thicker fillets of fish take longer to cook through.
Lower the heat and if the potatoes brown before the fillet
is cooked through, finish cooking it in a 350-degree oven.
A knife inserted in the center of the fish should feel warm
when touched carefully to your lip or wrist.*

MAKES 6 SERVINGS

SALT AND PEPPER

6 FILLETS OF SOLE (OR FLOUNDER), ABOUT 7 OUNCES EACH

2 EGGS, VERY WELL BEATEN

3 RUSSET POTATOES, GRATED (SQUEEZE THE WATER OUT OF THEM)

1/3 CUP VEGETABLE OIL

Salt and pepper each fillet and generously brush with the egg. Carefully press grated potato on the top of each fillet, covering it completely. Sprinkle a pinch of salt and pepper onto the grated potato. In a nonstick pan over medium heat, heat the oil, and when a pinch of butter dropped into the pan stops sizzling and disappears, add 2 or 3 fillets, potato-covered side down. When the edges of the potato are crisp and well browned, carefully turn the fillet and cook on the other side for about 2 minutes.

GARLIC-CRUSTED HALIBUT
WITH SALSA VERDE

*This is a perfect balance of crunch and salty
that halibut wears well.*

MAKES 4 SERVINGS

6 EGGS, WELL BEATEN

3 CLOVES GARLIC, FINELY MINCED

2 TEASPOONS SALT

1/2 TEASPOON PEPPER

2 TABLESPOONS BUTTER

1/4 CUP VEGETABLE OIL

FOUR 6-OUNCE HALIBUT FILLETS

2 CUPS DRY BREAD CRUMBS (PREFERABLY PANKO)

*Preheat the oven to 350 degrees. In a large bowl whisk the
eggs with the garlic, salt, and pepper. In a heavy-bottomed
skillet melt the butter into the vegetable oil over medium heat.
Dip the halibut in the egg mixture and let the excess drip off.
Coat the halibut in the bread crumbs. Brown each piece of
halibut in the pan with butter and oil. This should take about
4 minutes. Turn the pieces of fish and place the pan into the
oven. While the halibut is finishing in the oven, make the
salsa verde. It should take about 6 more minutes for the halibut to cook through.*

SALSA VERDE

MAKES 1½ CUPS OF SAUCE

1 CLOVE GARLIC

1 SMALL SHALLOT

2 CUPS FLAT-LEAF PARSLEY LEAVES, STEMS DISCARDED

1 TABLESPOON CAPERS

½ TEASPOON SALT

¼ TEASPOON PEPPER

1 CUP OLIVE OIL

1½ TEASPOONS ANCHOVY PASTE

JUICE OF 2 LEMONS

Blend the ingredients in a blender on high speed. Be careful not to blend the mixture too long. You want the sauce to remain bright green. Pour a spoonful of sauce on each plate and position the halibut over the sauce.

Eight

I'VE GOT TO BE ME

On my first day as chef of Mrs. Simpson's, I stood out of the way and watched as the staff put together a busy Sunday brunch. Maria, the only survivor of the original crew (she had started as a prep cook and by the time it was all over had been running the place), was browning French toast and filling blintzes. A server walked in—bow tie, tuxedo shirt, and yellowing guest check pad—shouting something above the hum of the equipment. I was finishing plates and watching for what I might change or leave alone as new chef, when I realized the shouting was for me to hear.

"Maria," he shot a glance at me, "as far as I'm concerned you are and always will be chef here."

"Thank you, Philippe," she said, smiling at him from the stove. She was rushing around like a madwoman but obviously having a good time. What had I walked into?

It turned out to be a difficult day. The kitchen wasn't particularly hot. Yet, before dinner service started I felt as if I needed to change out of my sweat-soaked chef coat. The kitchen staff glared at me and one of the waitstaff walked around me, snatching a pinch more chopped parsley to better complete the plate I'd just finished before carrying it out into the dining room.

During those first few weeks I felt toothless and insignificant, but I plugged away, disposing of the instant potatoes in dry storage and all of the bottled dressings in the cooler. The salad cook snarled at me but I kept putting plates in his fridge nonetheless. He had no choice but to comply and accept that the salad plates needed to be chilled. For a while I settled for these small victories. When he came in at 3:00 P.M. the first thing he'd do was count the plates in his fridge. I pretended not to notice when he'd add to the stack to make an even thirty.

It wasn't until Thanksgiving that I got the rest of the staff to start to call me Chef and treat me like one. With reservations in the triple digits and only one oven, I came in at 3:00 A.M. to roast the turkeys and the chestnuts. Maria stumbled in at 7:00 to bake the pies and start the ice cream. When the night was over, it was obvious that we'd done close to 150 covers. From 5:00 to 9:00 P.M., I'd put up ninety-five turkeys with dressing, thirty-six tenderloins with wild mushrooms, and twenty-two seared salmon. José dressed salads. Maria plated desserts. Both the front and back of the house could see that I wasn't just a clean chef coat and a dry towel.

"You're the expert," Mr. Bloomer had told me. He encouraged me to do what I needed to do in the kitchen. I changed the menu and reorganized the staff. I handled Maria carefully. Certainly she expected to come back to a kitchen where she could pick up right where she left off. She didn't expect a "real" chef to waltz into this building, where she had happily spent more than fifteen years, and tell her what to do. Maria showed herself to be a good cook. I let her continue doing the things that she thought made Mrs. Simpson's—the homemade ice cream, the Dutch apple pie, the little sugar cookies presented with the check.

It was what happened during a trip to the bathroom before she left for the day that made Maria my ally. She waited for Sian to come out of the single-stall employee lavatory. She could hear the water running and that just made it worse. The urge pounded at her innards so hard she crossed her legs at the ankles. But Sian was still in there washing her hands and singing. Maria waited and waited. Suppressing nature's call, she decided to hold it until she got home. That night she decided she could work with me. My daughter's singing was an unprovoked expression of real happiness. This girl's mother had to be a good person.

I had Maria baking and prepping during the week and let her have Sunday brunch. I opened the kitchen and unlocked the walk-in, helped her get started, and then I left. She could have Sunday to be chef at Mrs. Simpson's. Giving her this measure of control helped me get her to accept the new brunch menu.

I didn't interfere. I paused at the kitchen door one day and watched her. She stood in front of that stove in her trademark blue polo shirt and apron. The water for her hollandaise was boiling wildly and the oil in the pan for her French toast was smoking. The water sloshed onto the stove and slapped the oil out of the pan. Fire rushed up to the ceiling and the happy singing in Spanish stopped. I didn't move. I stood there and watched her from the door to my office. I figured I'd let her put out this fire by herself. She was by no means helpless. She had been running this kitchen before I got here. I left after she got it under control. I walked out as if I'd seen nothing. I never even asked her about the "old flavors." As far as I was concerned, they were old. These were the "old flavors" that lingered in the walk-in coolers until they grew stale. No one was coming to Mrs. Simpson's to sample those old flavors. The comeback of this restaurant would mean pushing the envelope to satisfy a more sophisticated Washington diner.

Things slowed down during the holidays, but as the New Year approached I recognized restaurant reviewers in the dining room. The much-needed reviews would bring more people into the dining room and help pay the bills. Bloomer was wringing his hands over the money. Why did I need all of this staff? Where was the money going? I knew he was concerned so I watched everything. When things were slow I sent staff home. I wrote personal checks for deliveries. I knew in my heart that our patience would be rewarded. My plan was to bring back those old customers and introduce new clientele to cutting-edge food. This restaurant was going to be one of those places where you needed reservations—and good luck trying to get one.

I was calm; I had been here before. I had sweated through the slow times at Evening Star. Back then our goals were simple. I remembered it took all summer before word got out and we made it past the ten-thousand-dollar month and were ringing up the ten-thousand-dollar week. Even Broad Street Grill seemed like a money pit at first. But the owner of Mrs.

Simpson's could see no light at the end of the tunnel. "Why do I have sixteen people working here?" he'd plead to the time clock. The time-card rack hanging on the wall seemed to barely contain the dozen cream-colored cards with names including Doug, José, Carlos, Wanda, Tomas, and Bernie. The cards flapped and fluttered like birds about to fly away. He'd look at the cards high above his head. To him, it was a tree full of wild birds from the Hitchcock movie and any minute they were going to swoop down on him and tear him to pieces.

I had no way of knowing that when I was hired that time-card tree was to be trimmed. I let it grow wildly out of control in my three months in charge. Mr. Bloomer envisioned just me and Maria working the line every night after spending the entire day prepping. His wallet could only fit a two-person kitchen staff, and the dishwasher made three. We didn't need to make desserts in-house. In fact Mr. Bloomer suggested his favorite bakery. At this little place, they mass-produced cakes and cookies using butterine. "When you have a restaurant of your own," he said, smirking, "you can do it the way you want." It was a preposterous notion—me having a restaurant of my own. He might as well have been suggesting that I was going to strike oil on Pennsylvania Avenue.

It took money and lots of it to have your own restaurant. One needed to have power and influence. I had none of that. Maybe I was a talented chef, maybe not. But that mattered little; without money and power I had to be content doing it everyone else's way but mine. It takes no time at all to stir up powdered mashed potatoes and bottled dressings. A scratch kitchen takes more hours and more staff. But Mr. Bloomer didn't understand that. Restaurants are not like a downtown office building bustling with attorneys and accountants. And when things don't taste the way they should, the chef pays for it in print.

It was my name on the menu, and I knew buying desserts from that bakery could ruin me. But it would have been a much easier decision if I hadn't already started to doubt myself. I certainly had had critical success as a chef at other restaurants, but was that enough? I had started at Evening Star in 1997, and it was just barely 2000. That was four chef jobs in four years. Maybe it *was* me. Was I letting my ego get in the way of being a team player? I wondered if I should approach things differently and just run the restaurant the way I was told.

I'd kept my fingers crossed and hoped the critics wouldn't notice me. I thought I might simply fade away into restaurant oblivion, but at least I would still have a job and be able to feed my kids and pay the rent.

So I cut staff and ordered desserts, choosing my job over my career. Well . . . as best I could and still sleep at night. I had my customers to consider. I did order desserts but I found a reputable company where a pastry chef friend had worked. My heels were dug in where the menu was concerned. Those old flavors were just not me. It would have been easier for me to master the cuisine of the Hunan Province.

My changes did little to ease the tensions. Mr. Bloomer would come into the kitchen snarling and looking about suspiciously even though there were considerably fewer time cards for his accountant to sort through. I posted our first review on the kitchen bulletin board. I photocopied it and handed it out to the servers at pre-shift meeting. The décor was politely called "as comfortable as an old friend's house," not stale and outdated. I reminded Leo that he was the server referred to as "welcoming and knowledgeable." He let his eyes drift up to me above his reading glasses. "Hmmm," he managed before looking down again. I was the only one excited. It didn't mean anything. Did they know something I didn't?

The good reviews were starting to have an effect in the dining room and in the reservations book. Now when the owners entertained their friends at the restaurant, I had trouble finding them in the crowded room. The pork chop with pear chutney arrived at the table followed by the seared duck breast. The Boswells, who were dining with the Bloomers, were dying to meet the chef. That's when I saw the faces—faces of dismay and disappointment that I had never seen before as a professional chef. Mrs. Boswell had to have the recipe for the pear chutney. I couldn't tell what Mr. Boswell had eaten . . . his plate was clean. But the Bloomers stared at their plates, poking at the seared duck breast sliced and fanned around a tiny cluster of fresh red currants. Before, I had shrugged it off when Mr. Bloomer smeared spicy brown mustard on my delicate jumbo lump crab cakes. I hadn't paid much attention when Mrs. Bloomer requested a sauce-less, side-less tenderloin, and "Just a slice of tomato with that, please."

That was one of the warning signs I was finding difficult to ignore: the owners of the restaurant where I was chef didn't seem to like my food. And they didn't care that there were people who did. I had a "huge" staff and together we spent the hours of the day concocting things in that kitchen that the Bloomers found nothing more than an embarrassment. The pressure was really on for me to do it his way. He was a man accustomed to having things the way he wanted them, and he trusted his own instincts over mine. A restaurant that served food he didn't like was not going to make it. That night I felt a pin prick my balloon. I started paying closer attention.

The nights can become a blur of smoke and steam when a restaurant gets busy. There's no way to tell if the mashed potatoes were perfection on Thursday or Wednesday night. There'll be a Friday night so busy that the tenderloin I'm ready to plate is nowhere to be found. I'll fire up another one on the fly. The next morning I'll find the lost portion of beef in the now cold oven. After twelve hours over the pilot light, it is now a piece of charcoal.

The slow nights we remember. On one slow Sunday at Mrs. Simpson's, there was plenty of time to clean the walk-in and the freezer. We wrapped the braised rabbits carefully in plastic wrap and stacked them in plastic bins. Sauces and dressings were poured into fresh containers. Foie gras was cut into four-ounce servings, wrapped with layers of parchment, and stored in the freezer. The grill was shut off and cleaned. The floor behind the stove was swept and scrubbed. We closed early and left quietly, knowing we had a clean kitchen to come back to on Tuesday morning and a light day of prep work.

In the meantime I'd become a morning person. While the girls were having breakfast at school I had my key in the door at Mrs. Simpson's. Before I flicked on the light I could tell something wasn't right. A bin of rabbit was warming on the windowsill. The cooler at the grill was open, with three portions of tenderloin on the floor. Foie gras melts like butter and was bleeding fat onto the grill. It was as if my kitchen had been hit by food-hating vandals. "Who did this?" I had an hour to clean it up before staff came in. I wanted whoever did this to know this little attempt at my undoing didn't work. To me it was a matter of scrubbing graffiti off a white wall.

Carlos was the first to come in, then Maria. They didn't notice anything suspicious. Doug went into the freezer to get the foie gras. "Why did I think there was more?" He scratched his head and shrugged. I was called out to sit down in the dining room with Mr. Bloomer and the manager. The kitchen was left a mess. There was food everywhere. What was I doing? The restaurant was going to lose everything because of my sloppy kitchen management. But how did they know about the mess? It had been cleaned before they'd arrived that morning; the spoiled food was in the Dumpster, and the foie gras fat was cleaned from the grill. Did these two in their suits and ties prance around the kitchen late Sunday night and pull my delicately braised rabbits into the danger zone? I shuddered. I promised to do better and went back to work. I was in the middle of something too strange to imagine and describe.

Could it be that there was now a campaign to kill me and make it look like suicide? I had no way of knowing for sure. I had crossed a line and I was barely clinging to the ledge. Whatever treachery may have been going on, was there anything I could do to stop it? I didn't even think the old flavors could save me. This was a boulder set in motion. It was the beginning of the end. It didn't matter how much I loved Mrs. Simpson. She didn't love me back. There was no point trying to change. She had seen me for what I was. I was someone she couldn't live with.

·   ·   ·

Pretending I was someone else was a way of life when I was a business executive doing the song and dance for the board of directors or a potential client. But in this new career I had gotten out of the habit of faking it. I wasn't good at it anymore. Now words and actions that weren't my own felt clumsy and not at all convincing. I hoped to save my daughters from having to make my mistakes and often suggested that they not follow the crowd and be themselves. But this is a difficult lesson to teach.

I often wonder if my kids would behave differently if I scattered pictures of myself around the living room. There's my sixth-grade class picture. I didn't smile because an accident at the pool had broken one of my front teeth. Then there's the one taken when I was sixteen, and my friends and I loaded one of those photo booths with quarters. Although only part of my face was showing you could tell that I was smiling. This was a big deal considering I had my hair cut the day before by someone who may as well have been a stylist for the circus. I swore I would wear a hat until graduation.

I wished I had saved the gym uniform that I had to wear all through junior high. It was the same uniform designed for the Great Neck North Junior High girls in 1954. Twenty years later, the girls' athletic department took pride in their adherence to tradition until the company that made the pale blue one-piece jumper went out of business. Ms. DiPalma had no choice but to authorize the change to the new coordinated T-shirt and shorts that the boys had been wearing. While the other girls in my class were excited to go to the campus store and buy the new-issue uniform that year, my parents didn't see the point. I was the only girl in the entire school still wearing the old uniform. My one-dollar-and-ninety-nine-cents sneakers completed the look.

I wanted the girls to know that I had lived many of the anguishes they feared and faced and that they weren't alone in their feelings of anxiety about their hair, clothes, and looks. But that was then. My broken tooth and bad-hair days didn't seem a match for the tragedies that they faced every day. They didn't believe me. Sometimes I think they really believed that I was never a teenager; that I was born with the calm and wisdom of an adult. Our age difference diminished my voice of experience. They couldn't imagine me wringing my hands over how important it is to have the right hair and the right clothes.

All of my "No, you don't want to do that," and "That's not going to work," or "Don't be silly, of course not" had no meaning. It was a lack of trust, a misguided certainty that stokes in the young mind and causes them to think, "Mommy has no idea what it's like. She couldn't possibly know that my survival in school depends on the right pair of jeans."

I must admit part of me wanted to protect them, to spare them the agony. Another part—the one they preferred, unfortunately—wanted to let go and let them see for themselves. Then there were the times they turned a deaf ear to my advice and stubbornly charged in the opposite direction. At seven, Sian decided she had all the answers. At eleven, Magalee had it figured out. As they became older, sometimes it felt as if I was just standing in the way of their destiny—as the school fashion standard, the resident psychic, or the miracle student who aced every exam without ever studying or doing homework.

Sian had always been well liked in school. Often the

smartest kid in the class, she was friendly with everyone and excluded no one. Her playground crew was an interesting combination of quiet girls, shy boys, and even the fast-developing ensemble who were full of charisma and labeled "popular." These popular girls were always trying to talk Sian out of her less charismatic friends.

Sian had those weak moments when she forgot herself and did the crazy thing that garnered "popularity." She could not refuse the invitation to the private club that met on the roof of the recreation center. The roof was the only place where this group of elementary-school children could talk about their schoolmates and not be discovered.

Sian went all year without having the "right" clothes. With nothing cool in her wardrobe, she had no choice but to improvise. What was it that all the pop stars were wearing this week? Flimsy camisoles. The closest thing Sian had in her closet was an undershirt. I picked her up from school to find her trying to hide her undershirt from me with a bright pink sweater.

These are powerless moments for a parent. How do you keep your child from doing what she knows is wrong? I shouted, knowing it was too late for that. I threatened, well aware that she had successfully carried out her plan. This was one of those times, however, that the lesson would teach itself. Sian had done the outrageous and unthinkable. She'd risked it all and worn a "camisole" to school. But nothing had changed. The popular girls treated her no differently—they were cold one day and friendly the next. The undershirt did not inspire awe in the quiet girls who swung with her on the monkey bars. Of all the people Sian knew, I'm the only one who remembers that she wore a "camisole" to school one hot day in June.

The struggle to find oneself is a difficult one for young teens and a trying one for their parents. This self-searching never ends, I've found, and it's good for teenagers to suffer through the first experience and get good at getting safely past the self-reflection, confusion, and ultimately on to self-definition. As parents, our function is to let it happen and set limits. Sure, they're changing and there are times we don't even recognize the stranger in our house who is going through puberty and struggling with a changing body and a growing mind. But they are suddenly struck with the need to make their own decisions. I found I would have had better luck trying to stop a runaway freight train than keeping my oldest from exercising her unearned independence.

Magalee started with an unannounced declaration that middle school would go much easier for her if she didn't bother with schoolwork. It did. Her afternoons were free and there was plenty of time for her to stare into space, read books that she had read in sixth grade, and draw pictures. It was worth it to Magalee. She had weeks of the freedom to spend her afternoons homework free, doing only what she felt like doing. All it really cost her was one or two hours of screaming and lecturing eight times a year (four parent-teacher conferences and the four report cards that followed).

There were birthday parties cancelled, trips abroad rescinded, and threats of military school. There were financial incentives of an additional five dollars' allowance for a week in which all work was turned in. I offered carrots including concert tickets in exchange for a report card with straight As. Nothing, neither positive nor negative reinforcement, encouraged Magalee to change her study habits.

I admired her determination, misdirected as it was. Here was a child who put energy into laziness. None of the usual things were working. And I wasn't sure if a change in her diet would do the trick or not, but I thought it was worth a try. I called it brain food. Magalee's diet was restricted to things such as seared salmon with lemon butter, spinach wilted in garlic olive oil, and roasted tomato and carrot soup. I hoped that a boost in iron and a reduction in sugars would stimulate her body chemistry to get her to think in a new direction.

I'd like to say that the brain food worked, that the spinach helped her think and the salmon gave her focus. It was probably a combination of things. There was increased attention to what proved to be a chronic problem with my oldest child. I was meeting with her teachers and in constant contact with them. I was also giving her work to do—book reports, math workbooks—homework from me if she swore she hadn't been assigned anything at school.

But on the brain-food diet, Magalee lost close to ten pounds and didn't spend the hours after dinner in a digestive stupor. The lighter meals kept her awake longer and enabled her to work later in the evenings to finish assignments that she had put off. Her complexion improved; she was lighter on her feet, physically more confident, and aware of her limitations.

I must admit, however, that it was Magalee's new high school, with its strict morning detention rules, that got her to put what she'd learned about herself into practice. A homework assignment that wasn't turned in earned the offending student morning detention an hour before classes started at 8:00 A.M. After the first missed assignment, I drove her to the school as the sun was coming up. It was the first and last time she'd be chauffeured. The three or four times that followed, she was up and out of the house at 5:30 in the morning to catch the bus and make it to detention on time.

Deprived of sleep and food she loved, Magalee soon became a great student. She was on top of her schoolwork, holding down a job bussing tables at the restaurant, and planning leisure time with her friends. She became a leader in her school and received academic awards in every subject. But Magalee was still a teenager. She and her friends, like hundreds of teenagers every day, decided to form a band and each of them took a stage name. Mag was to be known as Stupid Genius.

Pretty harmless, I thought, until the package came. Could it be the stuff circled in the catalog I'd confiscated? Knee-high vinyl platform boots adorned with a skull and crossbones were in the box for Stupid Genius. Before I showed her how to return an item for a refund, I asked Stupid Genius to wear her purchase down the stairs and sit down to dinner.

Sian and I waited at the dinner table for what sounded like Frankenstein's monster to make her way down to the dining room. The duck was getting cold, and the apple pie was out of the oven and cooling. By the time it was ready to cut, Stupid Genius was begging to get out of those boots.

After we ate I reminded the girls that the duck prepared the way I cooked it for them that night was the same as what I'd cooked for my boss at Mrs. Simpson's. Mr. Bloomer hated it, but this kind of food is what was in my soul and spirit. I couldn't cook duck his way. I think they understood. Some of the issues of their teen years would never really leave them.

There would come a time when they would finally feel comfortable with themselves. Questions, insecurities never really leave, however. As confident as you may be, there will be people who feed your insecurities.

No one knows how fast insecurities can multiply more than a chef does. A chef at a new restaurant has the same awkwardness and self-consciousness as a new kid in school. Will they like me? Should I cook French and fancy or just plain food?

Like a teenager, a chef wants to be accepted, noticed, and loved. You want the customers to understand you, to believe in you. It takes years of being a chef—of sometimes exposing yourself time and again to pain and disappointment—before you have the inner peace of a forty-year-old. It can take years.

While the chef and the teenager both always hold out hope for good reviews, they don't always come. After you've had a couple you realize a great review doesn't mean you'll be more loved or have more friends.

SPINACH WILTED IN GARLIC OLIVE OIL

Adding a little flavor to spinach always makes it easier for the kids to appreciate it.

MAKES 4 SIDE-DISH SERVINGS

2 TABLESPOONS PURE OLIVE OIL

2 CLOVES GARLIC, HALVED

1 SMALL PINCH SALT

1/2 POUND FRESH SPINACH

Heat the olive oil in a large skillet over medium heat. Brown the garlic halves in the olive oil and then remove them with a slotted spoon. Add the pinch of salt and then the spinach. Toss the spinach in the oil with a pair of tongs or a heat-safe spatula. The leaves will wilt and soften in about 1 minute. Transfer the spinach to a platter and serve immediately.

SEARED SALMON WITH LEMON BUTTER

Salmon is a popular fish but some diners are turned off by its strong flavor. Try slowly cooking it in the pan until there is a nicely browned, crisp crust and cooking it a little longer after you turn it. Serve it slightly above medium rare. Overdone salmon retains none of the sweet flavor. Instead it is overpowering and dry.

MAKES 4 MAIN-COURSE SERVINGS

2 TABLESPOONS VEGETABLE OIL

I TEASPOON BUTTER

FOUR 6-OUNCE SKINLESS FILLETS OF SALMON

I TEASPOON SALT

1/2 TEASPOON FRESHLY GROUND BLACK PEPPER

THE SAUCE

2 TABLESPOONS BUTTER

I SHALLOT, FINELY DICED

1/4 CUP WHITE WINE

GRATED ZEST AND JUICE OF 2 LEMONS

1 TABLESPOON HEAVY CREAM

1/2 CUP REALLY COLD BUTTER, CUT INTO CUBES

1/2 TEASPOON SALT

1/4 TEASPOON PEPPER

In a heavy-bottomed skillet heat the oil and 1 teaspoon butter until the butter stops sizzling. Season the salmon fillets with the salt and pepper. Place the salmon fillets in the hot oil on the bone side, and brown over medium heat. When the fillets are nicely browned, 8 to 10 minutes (you can see the edges crisp in the hot oil), turn and cook on the other side. Cook for another 10 minutes on low heat for medium-rare to medium salmon fillets. Set aside.

Heat the 2 tablespoons butter for the sauce over medium heat and add the shallots. Cook until the shallots start to brown at the edges. Pour in the wine, lemon zest, and juice. Bring to a boil and add the cream. Reduce the liquid until it is very thick and about one-third of the original volume. Add the salt and pepper. Off the heat, whisk in the cold cubes of butter. Whisk quickly and add the butter so that the mixture stays in a creamy emulsion. Strain the sauce and spoon a little evenly over four plates. Place the salmon on top of the sauce and serve immediately with the spinach.

ROASTED TOMATO AND CARROT SOUP

*Serve it hot with a grilled cheese sandwich or
chilled before the burgers come off the grill.*

MAKES ½ GALLON

1 POUND PLUM TOMATOES

1 TEASPOON OLIVE OIL

1 MEDIUM ONION, DICED

2 CARROTS, PEELED AND CUT INTO EIGHTHS

¼ CUP HEAVY CREAM

SALT AND PEPPER TO TASTE

SHREDDED CHEDDAR CHEESE FOR GARNISH

Preheat the oven to 400 degrees. Place the tomatoes in a baking dish and roast until the skin starts to pull away and tear and the tomatoes start to break and lose liquid, about 15 minutes. They should be very soft.

Heat the olive oil in a heavy 7-quart soup pot over medium heat. Cook the onions until wilted. Add the carrots and the roasted tomatoes. Simmer over low heat until the carrots are cooked. Remove the soup from the heat and, blend in batches, until very smooth. Return the soup to the soup pot and bring to a simmer. Add the cream and salt and pepper. Simmer until hot but do not allow it to boil. Serve with a garnish of shredded cheddar cheese.

SEARED BREAST OF DUCK
WITH RED CURRANT SAUCE
AND PARSNIP TURNOVERS

*Nothing complements the rich, slightly gamey taste
of duck better than the sweet and tart red currant.*

MAKES 4 MAIN-COURSE SERVINGS

THE DUCK

4 DUCK BREASTS (ABOUT 6 OUNCES EACH), SKIN SCORED AND
TRIMMED

SALT AND PEPPER

*Heat a heavy frying pan over high heat for about 5 minutes.
Season the duck with salt and pepper. Place the duck, skin
side down, on the blazing hot pan. It will immediately sizzle
and release fat. Turn the heat down to medium and continue
cooking the duck breasts until much of the fat is rendered and
the skin is nicely browned and crisp, 10 to 12 minutes. Pour
off the fat and return the pan to the stove over medium heat.
Cook the other side of the duck breasts for another 2 minutes
and set aside.*

THE SAUCE
(IF YOU CAN'T FIND CURRANTS, 12 OUNCES OF FRESH
CRANBERRIES WILL WORK)

MAKES 1 CUP OF SAUCE

2 PINTS FRESH RED CURRENTS (OR A 20-OUNCE PACKAGE OF
FROZEN RED CURRANTS OR PURÉE)

1/2 CUP SUGAR

I CUP RED WINE

SALT AND PEPPER

In a heavy-bottomed saucepan bring the currants to a boil
with the sugar and red wine. Simmer for 5 minutes and then
strain. Season with the salt and pepper.

THE TURNOVERS

MAKES 4 SIDE-DISH SERVINGS

I POUND PARSNIPS, PEELED AND CUT IN QUARTERS

1/2 CUP FINELY DICED LEEKS (WHITE PART ONLY)

I TABLESPOON BUTTER

2 TABLESPOONS HEAVY CREAM

SALT AND PEPPER

I PASTRY DOUGH FOR 9-INCH PIE

I EGG, BEATEN

In a 4-quart saucepan, boil the parsnips until tender. While
the parsnips are cooking, sweat the leeks in the butter until
they are wilted. Then add the cream and cook over low heat
for 2 or 3 minutes. Mash the parsnips through a food mill
into a large bowl. Blend in the warm cream and leeks. Season with salt and pepper. Allow this to cool.

Roll out the pastry dough and cut it with a round cutter
about 2 inches in diameter. You should have about 10 circles.

Brush each with beaten egg. Place a teaspoon of parsnip purée onto each dough circle just a little off center. Fold the dough over the purée and press the edges with a fork. Place all the turnovers onto a well-greased baking sheet and bake at 350 degrees for 20 minutes, or until brown all over.

APPLE-CRANBERRY CRUMB PIE

The texture of Braeburn apples is perfect for this pie. They soften and release plenty of juice when they're baked. The Braeburn is also sweet enough to stand up to the cranberries.

MAKES 8 LARGE SLICES OF PIE

2 TABLESPOONS BUTTER

1/2 CUP SUGAR

I TABLESPOON GROUND CINNAMON

8 APPLES, PEELED, CORED, AND CUT INTO EIGHTHS

1/2 TEASPOON SALT

I CUP FRESH CRANBERRIES

PREBAKED PIECRUST FOR 9-INCH PIE (LINE THE CRUST WITH FOIL AND WEIGHT IT DOWN WITH 1/2 CUP OF BEANS OR RICE AND BAKE FOR 5 MINUTES AT 475 DEGREES)

Preheat the oven to 375 degrees.

In a heavy, large frying pan, heat the butter, sugar, and cinnamon. Add the apples and cook, tossing frequently, over low heat. Cook until the apples begin to soften, 5 to 8 minutes. Toss in the salt and cranberries, then remove *from the heat. Pour the apple mixture into the prebaked piecrust.*

THE CRUMB TOPPING

2 CUPS OATS

1/2 CUP CHOPPED PECANS

1 CUP LIGHT BROWN SUGAR

1/2 CUP SOFTENED BUTTER

1 TEASPOON SALT

Combine all of the ingredients in a bowl and blend well with an electric mixer. Break into small clumps and cover the apples. Don't press the topping down or worry if there are spaces uncovered. The topping will melt and spread as it bakes. Place the pie in the center of the oven on a thin cookie sheet (it will ooze). Bake it for about 40 minutes. If the top begins to brown too quickly, cover it with foil.

Nine

BEING ME AND PAYING THE PRICE

It had been a week to the day after that slow Sunday night. Mr. Bloomer asked to see me in my office. It was a busy night and there was a lot to clean up and put away. I left my station a mess with food out and dirty towels. With the door shut behind him he looked down at his shoes and mumbled, "This just isn't working." He was nervous and timid as if he were telling me our affair had been a horrible mistake. It had to end now. I know men hate to end relationships because anything can happen. They have no idea how we women are going to react. To be honest, neither do we. I surprised myself when I sunk low in my high-backed office chair, grabbed the sleeve of his navy blue gabardine suit jacket, and begged Mr. Bloomer not to fire me. But it was Mrs. Simpson telling me to go back to Buckingham Palace. She didn't want me anymore. I made sob-choked promises, but it was too late. He looked down at me, disgusted, pulled his sleeve from my salty fingers, and left the room. I watched a pale blue folded paper float down onto my desk through tear-blurred eyes. There was nothing I could say. That little folded-up piece of paper was my check for the past week: six hundred sixty-seven dollars. It was the end of the fairy tale. I was chef at Mrs. Simpson's no more.

I remembered Sian looking at me one Monday night a few weeks before my dismissal. I had worked out the complicated staff issues yet felt there was something else still wrong. But it was something I could do little to change. It was me. I was obviously preoccupied when she asked me what was wrong.

"I don't think he likes my food."

"Don't be silly, Mommy." Magalee sort of sounded like me. "Everybody loves your food."

She was wrong. I was fired despite the great reviews that were pouring in and at the same time that reservations were darkening the books with ink. I was hurt, disappointed, and suddenly unemployed. But I could not be somebody I wasn't— a humorless, meat-and-potatoes maker who served tired-old-has-been-moth-eaten food like lamb with mint jelly. As ugly as it can get sometimes, both chef and teenager must find themselves and be themselves. I can only cook *my* food—use ingredients the way my brain and spirit move me to. My being fired was a great lesson for all three of us. None of us could really be somebody we weren't.

With very little in the bank I was staring at another major setback. It was feeling like a freefall now. Four chef jobs and four bad outcomes and it had only been four years. But I could not ignore the good reviews and the way the public reacted to what I created in the kitchen. The feeling was always in the back of my brain, the "what if." It gave me hope. Not what if another restaurant owner picked me in the next draft, but what if I could do what Mr. Bloomer had unknowingly dared me to do?

I found myself walking and driving by the same vacant storefront almost every day. I could see the small red-and-black FOR RENT sign taped to the window. One day I nearly rear-ended a school bus while I was looking at that sign. It was the perfect little storefront on Colorado Avenue. Two bay windows framed an old brick façade. A small sign above the door had turned gray. PASTA, INC. it read. Was this a spaghetti place that just couldn't hang on? There were no other restaurants in this part of Washington. Could one succeed now?

What started out as a setback could be an opportunity to follow Mr. Bloomer's advice: "When you have your own restaurant, you can do what you want." My own restaurant? At this point there didn't seem to be any other way. He was right. While I was working for someone else, I could never do what I felt was the right thing to do. There was no job security, anyway. Why not go out on a limb with a place of my own? I would have no less security, and at this point I really had nothing to lose. The fourteen hundred seventy-five dollars in my bank account was already spent on rent and aftercare. Owning my own restaurant was the only way to do this right and have a chance to really use my talents—to be a chef and in control. There would be no one to tell me the duck was too rare or that we needed to be serving a BLT in January. Here was the only way to succeed or fail on my own power.

There was no time to sit and stew. I called the number on the black-and-red sign. A man answered and agreed to meet me there in an hour. The space had housed a pasta wholesaler and then a storefront church. For $1,250 a month it could be mine. I headed downtown for the city paperwork and tax forms. I visited the Small Business Administration—the federal agency that assists small businesses with advice and loan guarantees—and made an appointment with a counselor. That night I circled the want ads and then sat down to write a business plan. I stalled and hedged about the rent and security deposit until I could get the last bit of cash out of my retirement account and borrow the rest. I didn't have much money but I had my name and reputation and a pile of press clippings. I had to make something out of it all. I certainly convinced the landlord. He had turned down several wide-eyed would-be chefs and gave me the keys to the vacant space. With the keys to this dusty store in my hands, I finally had control of my own future.

"You're going to do great here," the landlord assured me. The folks at SBA were equally encouraging. "We see a lot of people come in here with restaurant business plans. I have to admit I was prepared to tell you to think about some other business. But you've actually worked in a restaurant." He handed me a list of area banks. Mrs. Simpson's had tossed me out and taken my key. But I wasn't lonely for her anymore at all. Another door had opened. My friend Robin marveled at my ability to dust myself off and start over again. I told her and the girls over dinner one night that I was simply taking advantage of this opportunity to try another door. All I had to do was take it. Then I asked her for five thousand dollars. It would put a dent in the fifteen thousand dollars I needed to have in the bank for SBA to consider giving me a loan. There was the deposit for the equipment, and the architect needed two thousand dollars before he'd submit the plans to the city regulatory agency.

She wrote me a check for seven thousand dollars. "I have a feeling about this place," she said. "I want in."

The tiny commercial strip on Colorado Avenue was home to a humble assortment of neighborhood necessities. Each took the unimaginative route and named their establishment using their address. These stores had probably been around for as long as the oldest neighbor could remember. Colorado Cleaners had a twenty-foot-tall sign that helped it stand out like a pale blue sore thumb on the corner. Then there was Colorado Liquors—not only a place for the local winos to pick up a brown paper bag of sustenance, but also a place where just about everyone in the neighborhood picked up a lottery ticket. Even folks from the nicer houses drove by on their way from work to grab a bottle of wine to go with dinner.

When Robin and I walked up to our dark, quiet storefront and I put the key in the door, we knew what we had to call the area's first restaurant in twenty years—Colorado Kitchen. The name would instantly make us part of the neighborhood and make it seem like we'd been on the avenue forever, just like the other stores.

Using the word "Kitchen" in the name meant for me that the restaurant had to provide a dining experience that resembled a relaxed meal of comfort food taken at the kitchen table. My goal was to re-create the kitchen table meals at my grandmother's house. We never ate around the table in her formal dining room. The stemware and candelabra were in that other room. That didn't matter. Nana's soup was best served at her chrome-banded kitchen table with the yellow vinyl chairs.

But comfortable or not, making Colorado Kitchen was going to cost money. Right now I was unemployed and the restaurant I was planning was one more mouth to feed. Collecting unemployment wasn't going to cut it. I needed a job.

While the interviews went well, I never got a callback. Line-cook and salad station jobs, deli-counter cashiers—I never made it to the drug test. That's when I just had to ask the human resources manager at the hotel where the chef, so excited that someone at the job fair could make hollandaise, had basically shown me my locker. "We called the folks at your last job," she'd confessed.

I had finally caught her at her desk after ringing right into voice mail for a little over a week. I trusted the sugary singsong voice on the recording and just knew that she'd be answering my detailed message. I left one every day. "They told us that you were fired because you were letting food spoil." In my mind, she was sitting there at her dark walnut desk amid huge, neatly stacked sheets of paper, pinching the phone to her ear with her shoulder. In her hands was my resume, the word LIAR rubber-stamped in bright red. My lips were moving and sound was coming out, but the air had been knocked out of me. I hadn't the strength to defend myself. She probably thought my incoherent babbling was muttered swear words. She hung up on me.

Was Mrs. Simpson bent on ruining me? At this rate I'd never cook in DC again. She sure was making it hard to forget about her and move on. I had no choice but to pretend the winter of 1999 hadn't happened.

The omission on my resume landed me at Hogate's, a waterfront seafood establishment that for years was DC's top seafood restaurant. Hogate's had seen better days. Buoyed by its reputation, the old place still fed lunch and dinner to hundreds of tourists. Locals crowded in during the Sunday brunch buffet for waffles and made-to-order omelets. I became one of the highest-paid line cooks and the only girl on the hot side. "Don't let any of them know how much you're making," the chef said, handing me a polyester chef coat with bright plastic buttons. "These guys are old-school. They won't get it." He looked at my chest and took the coat back. "I'd better go in the back and get you a forty-two."

It was one of those kitchens that I'd only heard stories about. The staff could cook the thirty-year-old menu with their eyes closed. The building was old and breaking away on the inside in chunks. Roaches fell out of the ceiling tiles and into salads headed for the dining room. Sewer gas floated up from the floor drains. On really hot days when the air was heavy and didn't move much, the gas was ignited by the burning wood in the grill. Flames swirled around us behind the line. The waterfront location contributed to the rampant rat population.

"We have city squirrels," the chef warned me while he shut the door to walk-in number seven. When I settled into my spot behind the fryers I checked my station fridge and found an army of roaches ambling over my stuffed clams and crab cakes. José patiently showed me how to set up the station for lunch. "Like this," he told me. He took the big knife out of my hands to show me how he cut broccoli. "Uh oh." He sucked saliva through clenched teeth. He took the cashews out of the cold oven (it hadn't worked in years). The container hadn't been covered. "I have to throw these away now." He shook the bucket of nuts so I could see the checkerboard effect of dark brown roach and tan cashew. José showed me how to carefully pull the string from the snow peas. He used the tip of his paring knife to flick the dirt from the crease of a red bliss potato, stressing to me how important it was with a little demonstration of how a customer might bite down and feel the grit in his teeth. As far as José was concerned, I had never cooked a day in my life. And if I was going to spend my days working beside him putting out lunch at Hogate's, I was going to do it all his way. In the midst of all of this filth and vermin infestation, José had a standard. I wish I had a nickel for every time I was in the middle of dicing an onion or loading *mise en place* on a cart only to hear José's "No, no. Like this."

The rest of the staff was reckless and undisciplined. My chef coat, boots, knives, and aprons were all eventually stolen. The on-site laundry was not only a convenient alternative to the expensive linen services, but also the perfect place for the utility staff to host its sex parties.

On late nights as I rushed through my part of cleanup so that I could hurry home to relieve the babysitter, Won Cha, the sauté cook, would call out to me, "Hey, where are you going? Take your time and make some money." The rest of them washed down their stations past midnight, milking the clock and scoring overtime. The place had become one of those subculture kitchens. Once I walked through those staff doors I entered a world where the laws of civilization didn't apply.

Sometimes I was shifted over to run the kitchen at the BBQ place next door. With a cigarette dangling from her lips, Carla would set me up by piling flour-dredged chicken into the fryer. With heavy lids at half-mast, she shuffled around the huge kitchen like an insomniac, dumping ribs, burgers, and sauces at my station. She opened her eyes just a little bit wider and turned on the grill. I had about a ten-inch-square surface of hot grill to work on. The rest of the four-foot charbroiler was caked with years of food soil so thick the flames didn't penetrate.

"Call me if the tickets get too crazy and you need some help back here," she said. Ashes floated to the floor. She pulled a big swallow of air and the end of her cigarette glowed red-hot before she went back to the big glass-walled office the *sous*-chefs shared.

I kept my eyes on the prize. There was no other way to work in that nightmare of a kitchen thirty-five hours a week. Knowing that it was temporary helped me make it through the days. When I could sneak out early, I'd head over to the store and scrape some of the old paint off the tin ceiling that we were hoping to restore and paint Ralph Lauren Golden Candlesticks. On a Saturday afternoon, simply because the bidding contractors were having trouble understanding the flow of the room, Robin and I used a circular saw and a hammer to bring down a wall.

I was itching to move the project along but knew that feeding the kids and paying for seventeen tables and fifty chairs meant I had to spend my days demonstrating grills at local hardware stores and my nights deep-frying breaded clams.

After work, when the kids were in bed, we'd visit the

empty space. My voice bounced off the bare walls as I showed Robin where finished plates would be picked up and where the dish machine was going. We spent hours visualizing and fantasizing and crossing our fingers. There was no way of knowing that all of this hard work was going to pan out. There were restaurants close to me that were having to regroup. I heard through the grapevine that Mrs. Simpson's was struggling— that with all of his money, Bloomer wouldn't be able to save it. Broad Street Grill had been sold and was pretty much a bar now. The menu was almost entirely coming out of the fryer. I was staying busy with multiple jobs and working out details in the vacant room, and it kept the jitters away.

But I couldn't get used to it—the rats running around the perimeters of the kitchen and dining rooms, me shielding my eyes when getting a fresh stack of towels from the laundry to avoid seeing heaps of stinky trash going out the same loading dock as the produce came in. I walked out of Hogate's one day and never went back. I was lured away by the promise of better pay and free uniforms with a *sous*-chef job at a conference center. The uniforms would come in handy; one less expense for the chef at Colorado Kitchen just months away from opening. With a forty-thousand-dollar-a-year salary there'd be even more money to pay for the things the bank had left for me to cover. As the *sous*-chef of this busy kitchen, making lunch for meetings and dinners for the ballroom, I was supposed to be running the show. But I found myself struggling to fit in. I felt as if I had abruptly enlisted as an officer in the German army. I knew neither the rules nor the language. Recipes came from a faraway headquarters and by the time they got to the big white binder in the office, they were indecipherable. There were blurry photos of the final outcome. There were words like *à la nage* and *puttanesca* but no list of ingredients. Roulades—filled with a mystery stuffing—were to be sliced and fanned on specified dishware we didn't have. It was a culinary game of telephone. Plus I had Laurel and Joanne to contend with. These two women saw an enemy when their eyes landed on me. Somehow there was a chance I might stand in the way of their advancement in the chain. Too many times I stepped on a land mine with my Professional Birki Clogs.

"Where's Laurel?" I asked Merle, who had just been promoted from the prep kitchen to help steam vegetables and grill chicken breasts for the banquet kitchen.

"She called in sick." Merle winced. "It's just you and me. We have two hours to prepare for the party and the produce isn't here yet." There was a quiver in her voice. I was afraid she was going to start crying again. Last week Joanne, the lead banquet cook, had reduced her to tears when the parsleyed potatoes were underdone.

Too often "mistakes" on the schedule showed my shift ending at 4:00 P.M. and a party starting at 6:00 with no one else on the schedule. "We're going to start serving the soup at six-fifteen," the call would come to the kitchen. I'd pick up the girls from aftercare, hurry back to the kitchen, and have only an hour to heat the soup and roast off the Wellingtons. Laurel, the assistant *sous*-chef, had been cranking out the weekly schedule for years, but only made these manpower errors on her days off and when Joanne was taking a vacation day. Laurel had been working in that busy kitchen for years and with the benefit of her experience knew which weeks to avoid. She scheduled me for the morning shift on the days the youth club came for their annual week of morning meetings. On these mornings I arrived before sunup and ran around cooking and loading hot boxes with scrambled eggs and bacon for one hundred and fifty. At the same time I had to boil grits and oatmeal for the cafeteria. I managed to survive every grenade hurled my way and still had time to use my company-issued cell phone to check up on contractors. There were afternoons when my long walk across the campus after lunch led me straight to the parking lot and I snuck away to meet the building inspector or the health department.

There was poison on the tip of the sword the day I came in and found fifty pounds of frozen shrimp in a metal-banded crate in the walk-in. "Albert ordered the wrong shrimp," Rosa said, walking toward me and tightening her hair net. "We were supposed to get the frozen peeled and deveined shrimp already cooked and seasoned." She walked with me back into the cooler and pointed to the crate. "We need thirty pounds." She was clasping her latex-gloved hands together. "Laurel brought these up from the freezer. This frozen raw shrimp is all we have." I pounced on the crate before Rosa could tell me all about how she didn't know what to do and that ladies in the prep kitchen were not allowed to go near the stove—company policy. The metal bands were off and I had six of the ten boxes in the sink with hot water coursing down on them. I put the biggest pot I could find on to boil with water, white wine, cayenne, garlic, parsley, and thyme. I ran a filleting knife on the stone until it was scalpel sharp and could cut through the shell and slice the shrimp open at the vein in one stroke. What Joanne and Laurel didn't know was that I had suffered many nights alone at Evening Star Café and had run out of mashed potatoes in the middle of service countless times at Broad Street Grill. Joanne was sticking around past her clock-out time to slice ham for tomorrow's lunch buffet. Laurel was manager of the day that night and came by the kitchen to pick up her walkie-talkie. I hardly noticed them. I was plunging pound after pound of cleaned and poached shrimp into a tub of ice water. I had soaked my sleeves to the shoulder and had sloshed court bouillon all over my ankles. It was quite a performance. But Rosa had her shrimp.

Joanne plucked off the stems, scraped away the brown feathers, and peeled all the character from a case of portobello mushrooms. Merle noticed me watching the precious pounds of mushroom fall into the trash can. "She saw it on the television," Merle said as Joanne proudly put her portobello-turned-white-button mushrooms on a sheet tray to roast. Next she tackled the crab cakes. Pound after pound of jumbo lump was stirred vigorously into a blend of mayonnaise and cayenne. The lumps were pounded into stringy strands that resembled claw meat. I started to say something. She was working fast, dumping in pounds of bread crumbs and then shaping the mixture with a tiny ice cream scoop and plopping the "crab cakes" into the fryer. She couldn't hear me clear my throat over the rush of boiling fryer oil.

"No bay leaf," Laurel said. "That's against the rules." She tossed the box of dry leaves—a choking hazard if not handled properly—I'd ordered for the bouillabaisse. Out went the fresh thyme and chives as well. "Headquarters forbids all fresh herbs." She smiled at me. One more thing she knew that I didn't. "They can't be washed properly." I was on another planet. Everything I knew and believed about food was wrong here. This was never more apparent than when I interpreted the event instructions and made something from scratch— mashed potatoes, chicken stock, or soup. The morning I emptied ten pounds of asparagus trimmings into the soup kettle I got plenty of suspicious stares from the staff. Richard, the stressed-out cafeteria cook charged with preparing the cafeteria lunch special, looked at me with wide-eyed disbelief. "What are you doing?" I sweated the bits of asparagus with onion and a little olive oil. "Did we run out of frozen soup concentrate again?" He shook his head. "Man, they got you making soup from scratch. Can you believe this?"

Joanne and Laurel sneered at my soup. Of course it was gone before lunch had been served to everyone and there was none for the cafeteria. I was heating the boil-in-a-bag broccoli and cheddar on the fly. I couldn't win.

Maybe because I knew my time in this kitchen was limited, I was content with being an outsider. If this had really been my kitchen, I would have challenged the dominatrix pair. Corporate kitchens make it easier for supervisors to get their way. Memos would have been written and anyone who continued to peel off the best part of the portobello would be written up. Instead, I smiled at Joanne and let her do her mushroom thing. I handed Richard a rubber spatula and watched him stir cold milk over the potatoes as they were whipped tough in the sixty-quart mixer. I sprinkled dry, tasteless chives on the potatoes au gratin, and did a whole bunch of other things that made me cringe inside.

I was laughing a belly-shaking laugh at the joke with no punch line. You know, the one that we've all told to the new kid to see if he laughs just to fit in or if he is bold enough to say, "I don't get it," and earn our respect forever.

Sian, separated from her elementary-school cronies when I enrolled her in a private middle school, found herself saying "I don't get it" to the well-established cliques at her new school. She spent a lonely sixth-grade year not getting the joke and not going to playdates.

She was encouraged by the magazines she was reading at the library—all of them full of lessons in throwing parties. There were features to help you get and be the Best Friend Forever. She followed the fashion do's and don'ts as if it were a religion. Those magazines and cosmetics advertisements were the keys and secrets to being the "it" girl. Sian began her seventh-grade year determined to be popular. There was much to overcome, however. Sian wasn't raised like many of these children. She had spent a great many years in the kitchens and dining rooms of restaurants where the grown staff members treated her like one of the gang.

It wasn't unusual for Sian to put on an apron and pitch in. With more than half of my staff on vacation, I put Sian on a milk crate one week at Broad Street Grill. She was now tall enough to handle the stand mixer and was able to blend the yolks one at a time for the mixed berry clafoutis or the *pâte à choux*. A busy Sunday brunch and no dishwasher found Sian again standing on a milk crate so she could load plates into the dish machine. She took a break from bussing tables on a suddenly busy Wednesday night so I could pull out a loose baby tooth with a kitchen towel. It is no wonder that the school principal and teachers were some of Sian's favorite people in the little school building uptown. She spent much of her developing years elbow to elbow—in what we call the trenches—with grown folks.

The other kids noticed this curiosity about Sian way before she did. During a class discussion late in the school day when talk often strays a bit from the standard curriculum, Sian volunteered that Bette Davis's character in the classic film *What Ever Happened to Baby Jane* was an excellent example of a person who did not have a firm grip on reality. Mr. Kane thought Sian's answer was insightful and beyond her years. Score one more point in his book—yes, she was up there on his list of kids he'd remember long after eighth-grade graduation. The rest of the class groaned. She was over their heads again, saying something crazy that only Mr. Kane would understand. The groans and whispers were deflating to Sian and may have tempted her to hide or rearrange her true self.

As much as I fought her on these things, I knew what she was going through. I let her pick out her own outfit to wear to the spring dance. She headed to the mall with the gift card she got for Christmas with so much hope in her eyes it made me nervous. She modeled the outfit for me before bedtime that night. The skirt was a little on the too-short side and the top was tight as far as I was concerned. This was perhaps a time to loosen the reins. The foundation for popularity and lasting friendships was being laid. I let her wear the outfit to the dance, so "for just this once," she could be like the other girls in her class.

But I refused to allow Sian to let judgmental preteens have too much control. I told her that her band teacher needed her more than they did. There was no way she was quitting the saxophone. I succeeded in convincing a girl bent on being not just one of the gang, but "popular," that she would remember the great fencing victory during her last match as a senior long after she'd forgotten the names of the girls she was trying so hard to impress. So I signed her up for the fall session of fencing class, though the girls at school would surely die if they knew Sian was making great progress in manipulating the épée.

There were things I knew about Sian that these girls would never know. I saw the smile on her face when she nailed her solo. Performing in the concerts meant more to her than an opportunity to wear heels. It gave her a thrill she could not describe. When she was able to get her body to do all her coach said and score a touch while sparring with a fellow fencing student, inside a victory dance went on.

It's near impossible to get Sian to see herself as I see her and accept it. She will always want to wear something different, want different hair, and not want to wear her glasses. I can only hope that the drive to constantly remake herself will mature and channel into something positive. I hope it makes her want to be a better student, musician, athlete—a better person. Being herself meant some difficult middle-school years, but as much as she tried to keep it under wraps, Sian couldn't help but show everyone around her who she is.

There was no better example to set for Sian than opening Colorado Kitchen. From the beginning I made it clear that this restaurant would be inflexible in its adherence to my approach to food. This restaurant, unlike all of the others where I'd worked, would be mine; it would be me. Four walls and floor-to-ceiling me. There was no room for faking or pretending. Colorado Kitchen would be my food memories and feelings—the product of my experiences.

When we got close enough, I finally left the conference center. I took a long walk across campus, over the grassy hills and into the parking garage, and snuck out. The building inspector was coming for a final look. In two weeks we would open the doors of Colorado Kitchen. There was a lot to get done. The tin ceiling was to be painted gold and the black-and-white floor tiles had to be glued down. I gave the girls rollers and white enamel and had them put a fresh coat on the cinder blocks in the basement storage area. For Sian especially I thought it important to involve them in the project from the beginning. I wanted them to begin contributing immediately. We'd be spending a lot of time in this building. There was no better way to instill in them a sense of ownership. It was important for my daughters to contribute and feel a part of the family business, especially when the crowded hallways at school could be a lonely place.

After the stove arrived, whatever was left from recipe testing was just fine for our family dinner. We'd prop the door open to lessen the smell of paint or floor adhesive and, until the furniture arrived, pull up buckets to the prep table and eat on paper plates. Having dinner was and always will be an opportunity for my family to let the air out. We could defuse the tension of a day at school or a day in the kitchen by sitting down together. It could be delivery pizza, a roasted chicken, or the teriyaki pork chops my mother taught me how to make. What mattered was that it was like time in the locker room with our own team. Whether we were celebrating a win or rubbing away the sore of a loss, dinnertime was not only a half hour of enjoying the company of those who knew us best, but also a time to plan a strategy or a new angle of attack. The next day we could go back to school or to work stronger.

PINEAPPLE UPSIDE-DOWN CAKE

*Our signature dessert at Colorado Kitchen, but,
at first, slow to catch on. We made the dessert
a sensation by promoting "the coveted corner piece"
on tabletop advertising.*

MAKES 6 DESSERT SERVINGS

THE TOPPING

1/2 CUP BUTTER

1/2 POUND LIGHT BROWN SUGAR

1/4 CUP PINEAPPLE JUICE

6 CANNED PINEAPPLE RINGS

3 MARASCHINO CHERRIES, CUT IN HALF

THE CAKE

10 TABLESPOONS BUTTER

1 CUP SUGAR

2 TEASPOONS PURE VANILLA EXTRACT

2 EGGS

2 CUPS FLOUR

1/2 TEASPOON SALT

2 1/2 TEASPOONS BAKING POWDER

1/2 CUP PINEAPPLE JUICE

1/2 CUP MILK

Heat a 9 × 5-inch glass baking dish in the oven at 350 degrees. Add the butter to the warm dish. Remove the dish from the oven when the butter has melted. Stir in the brown sugar and pineapple juice. Arrange the rings of pineapple in the sugar mixture in two rows of three. Fill the center of each ring with a cherry half. Set this aside to cool and set.

In a stand mixer, cream the butter and sugar. Add the vanilla and eggs. In a separate bowl, sift together the flour, salt, and baking powder. Add the wet mixture to the dry ingredients. Stir in the pineapple juice and milk. Stir gently to form a lumpy but well-incorporated batter. Pour the batter over the topping in the dish. Bake in a 350-degree oven for 35 minutes, or until a toothpick pricked into the center of the cake comes out clean.

Cool for 5 minutes, and then invert the cake on a large cutting board or platter. Allow to cool for 10 minutes more before cutting.

TERIYAKI PORK CHOPS WITH FRIED RICE

*I learned to make this while watching my mother carefully make
tiny cubes of garlic with a paring knife and stir the
brown sugar into the soy sauce in a bone-white coffee cup.*

MAKES 4 SERVINGS

¾ CUP DARK BROWN SUGAR

I TABLESPOON MINCED GARLIC

I TEASPOON FINELY CHOPPED FRESH GINGER

I CUP SOY SAUCE

½ TEASPOON SALT

I TEASPOON FRESHLY GROUND BLACK PEPPER

I TABLESPOON COOKING OIL

FOUR 8-OUNCE PORK CHOPS

Preheat the oven to 375 degrees. Blend the sugar, garlic, ginger, soy sauce, salt, and pepper together in a heavy-bottomed saucepan. Simmer for 5 minutes over low heat until the sugar is dissolved and the garlic is very soft. Heat the oil in a frying pan over medium-high heat. Add the chops and brown on both sides. Pour the excess oil from the pan and discard. Coat each chop with the sauce and transfer the coated chops to a baking sheet. Bake in the oven for 30 minutes.

THE RICE

1 TABLESPOON COOKING OIL

1 LARGE ONION, THINLY SLICED

2 LARGE EGGS, BEATEN

3 TABLESPOONS SOY SAUCE

2 CUPS COOKED WHITE RICE

1 TEASPOON SALT

1/2 TEASPOON FRESHLY GROUND PEPPER

Heat the oil in a frying pan. Add the sliced onion and cook over medium heat until wilted. Add the beaten eggs and stir vigorously. When the eggs are cooked, stir in the soy sauce and then the rice, salt, and pepper. Toss the rice with a large spoon or fork.

Ten

PLENTY OF CHANCES TO LEARN FROM MISTAKES

Colorado Kitchen—from concept to completion—took nineteen months to build. With my full-time cooking job and part-time grill-demo gig along with Robin's full-time job in customer support and part-time work as a mystery shopper, we were able to funnel over twenty-three thousand dollars into the project. There was plenty of time waiting for the SBA loan to be approved. Robin and I bit our nails while the city pored over our plans to convert the storefront to a full-service restaurant with the required bathrooms and fire exits. We had twelve hundred square feet of first-floor space to work with. The kitchen and service areas were my design. Small and efficient, the kitchen would be open. Everything that happened to food at Colorado Kitchen could be seen from the street, to say nothing of the dining room, if the lighting was right. The kitchen just fit a six-burner stove and two fryers with a small table by the step-in cooler for rolling out dough and for cream-ing butter and sugar in the stand mixer. It would take seven months for the contractor to finish a job he had estimated would take his crew a little under eight weeks to complete. This left plenty of time for us to shop the thrift and antique stores for old magazine advertisements and vintage china.

We had decided that there was no better way to make Colorado Kitchen feel friendly and accessible than to serve food on plates that weren't the standard restaurant warehouse issue. We used images of classic food advertising—those icons of the forties and fifties that came to symbolize America's burgeoning food culture. The images of Aunt Jemima, the Pillsbury Doughboy, Rastus, Mrs. Butterworth's, and others were framed and hung to help customers recall their food memories when entering the dining room, patterned after the dining area in my grandmother's kitchen. Aunt Jemima's bandana became the symbol of our commitment to feeding people. Black, white, and red were the colors of our floor, walls, and chairs. We bought hundreds of red bandanas to serve as napkins. The final touch—after we'd painted the ceiling gold, the chair rail red, and glued down the black-and-white floor tiles—was to affix a hat rack to the wall. We hung chef hats and a single bandana as if to say, "They're here."

While we worked on the space late on weeknights or early on weekends, the door was often pushed open. It was another vagrant. This one reeked more of stale beer than of urine. He, too, had three teeth and needed a job. When we first took on the project the landlord told us stories. He and his siblings had acquired this and other properties from their father's estate. The store was built in 1904 and was one of three stores in the residential neighborhood. The first mom-and-pop markets were long gone. He'd rented it to storefront churches and African clothing boutiques. No one held on for very long, although the drug dealing had slowed down and the cars that often were crashed up onto the sidewalk and abandoned were no longer a problem. The neighborhood was changing. The building owner was convinced that we were just what Brightwood needed.

I looked around and saw what I had seen on so many streets in the nation's capital. It was a black neighborhood that struggled to get police and retailer attention. Many of the residents fought what was going on in the streets, but even more had given up. The lower house prices were attracting caring citizens who could not afford to buy in the neighborhoods with better reputations. The base of residents that wanted the neighborhood back was growing. Looking out from the big glass windows, I witnessed occasional drug deals and at times had my view spoiled by graffiti. It wasn't enough to stop me from opening a business on the site. As I saw it, things were looking up in Brightwood. We were just part of the wave of improvement. Surely there were more people like Robin and me, who saw the low rent and proximity to so many neighborhoods as an opportunity. Yet we were indeed alone. No full-service restaurant had opened in the area since the early seventies. There were plenty of places to get a sub or a single beer passed to you through bulletproof glass. There was no place like Colorado Kitchen. Our focus was access and openness. The first thing we did when we took possession of the building was to remove the security bars from the windows and door. A restaurant can't have security excess and atmosphere at the same time. Until our sign went up, there was no place in

Brightwood to sit down and be served. There was no Starbucks and no other restaurant with cloth napkins. For many in the neighborhood we were a symbol of change; for real-estate agents we were a key to selling a single-family home.

The ambitious renovation of the space that would be Colorado Kitchen drew considerable interest. The neighborhood was buzzing even though newspaper was taped over the big bay windows. Curious onlookers were never too shy to open the door and ask questions. When the newspaper was taken down and the protective plastic was taken off the chairs, many of our neighbors came in looking for work.

There were high-school kids and older folks from the nearby apartments. Robin worked with the kids we hired for the dining room. With help from servers I'd worked with at Broad Street Grill, she fought the uphill battle of trying to get a totally inexperienced staff to polish silverware and refill water glasses. The concept of serving an appetizer before the main course was pretty complicated to a segment of the population that subsisted on Chinese carryout. Many of these kids had never eaten at a restaurant. There was a huge learning curve.

In the small kitchen, I practiced with a crew that wasn't much different from the talent I'd had to work with at my first chef job at Evening Star Café. Many found the kitchen intense. There was room for only two (at a hot and a cold station) to crank out food for a dining room that eventually fed 175 diners on a busy Saturday. The menu would change often but was smaller than the long lists of food I produced at other spots. Training staff to grasp a few core items and adapt to the menu changes was relatively easy, and most everyone I hired could identify with meatloaf and biscuits. They had each cut a chicken into its eight parts before, too.

We all managed to struggle through a few days of training that culminated in a Friday night mock service—invited guests got to order off the menu, simulating a moderately busy night. The waitstaff got the opportunity to work out the kinks of order taking, timing, entering orders into the POS (point of service) system, and delivering food. The kitchen staff was able to practice preparing and plating the studied menu for real live customers. We were as ready as we'd ever be to finally open.

It was cause for the *Washington Post* to cover our opening day. Our first service was brunch on Sunday, July 29th, 2001. It was busy and we were, despite all of our planning, terribly disorganized. We'd hired an inexperienced but ambitious crew of neighborhood kids to serve as waitstaff and old hands that had worked at Broad Street Grill and Evening Star to help us make it through a day when we knew from experience just about anything could happen.

The press snapped photos and interviewed neighbors who had been peeking through the papered windows to gauge our progress. They said it was great to have a restaurant they could walk to. Many had come in asking for rye toast with their eggs; some folks wanted whole wheat. But when servers explained that there was no toast, that Colorado Kitchen served these little homemade biscuits, they were met with angry looks. A few who walked out in disgust, shouting that they would not be back, didn't understand that a commercial toaster in the little kitchen was a safety hazard.

We fed sixty people that morning. It was busy enough to give us an opportunity to see what needed work. There needed to be a better system of handling dirty dishes. Loose silverware set on the table turned out to be a fiasco. The fastest and easiest way to get tables ready for the volume was to roll the salad and dinner forks and a knife tightly in a bandana. We had two hours to sweep up and turn it around and greet the dinner crowd. It got darker and darker outside. Colorado Avenue was quiet. I kept the stove on and pans hot while we waited for customers. The servers read the paper and the busboy dozed on a bar stool. Finally the door swung open. Robin, menus in hand, went to greet our first dinner customers and show them to a table. They paused at the door, a little unsure about this white woman and what she was talking about. They continued and stopped at the counter. They looked around but there was no posted menu. "Isn't this a soul food carryout?" No, they were told. They looked around once more before leaving, not appreciating our decorative touches, disgusted that they'd be settling for the Chinese carryout on Georgia Avenue.

We were being typecast by our surroundings. What else would open its doors in this neighborhood but a soul food carryout? This was a few square miles of liquor stores, storefront churches, greasy spoons, fried chicken shacks, and Chinese carryouts. Surely someone serving classic American cuisine with table service and no carryout menu would have the good sense to open a store somewhere downtown. Would we have to serve soul food to survive in this neighborhood? Hadn't Donna, the one-eyed crack addict, read our sign and declared, "You better be serving neck bones if you gonna call yo'self a kitchen"? For the first time in twenty months, I was scared. I sat at table fifteen in the back, near the door to the kitchen, and the weight of a seven-year lease and a loan for one hundred ten thousand dollars started to make my knees buckle. I shuddered and started to quietly sob.

I didn't want the girls or the staff to see me losing it, but I was inconsolable. Nothing Robin said could bring me out of it. I was convinced that we would be either shutting our doors or serving neck bones. Then the door swung open and out of the dark a young couple entered our brightly lit dining room. They were smiling and looked happy to be at Colorado Kitchen. We cooked our hearts out for them. Our signature pineapple upside-down cake topped off their meal. They were very pleased and swore they'd be back. I was suddenly relieved and with the door locked we cleaned the kitchen, laughing and joking about our first day.

We had decided to close on Mondays. But when we drove up early Monday morning after our quiet Sunday night, there was a crowd at our door. We pushed through the curious mob and let ourselves in. The phone was ringing. Mrs. Fleming had followed us through the throng of people asking questions and anxious to come in. She had the morning paper in her hands. Someone had left it in her Laundromat across the street. "I was about to throw it in the trash." She was smiling and had the paper open on the counter. "Then I turned to this page and saw your picture." There I was in the kitchen. Roshena (she had been my right hand two other times and I figured I could get a couple of good years out of her) was in the background. We were the featured story of the Metro section.

To be honest, we were so involved in making the restaurant work on Sunday that we forgot all about the reporter and photographer who were circulating the dining room. The phone didn't stop ringing. Robin and I took turns answering it, repeating the restaurant hours over and over again. For a week the crowds came and the phone rang. There were radio interviews, and regular citizens brought in milk and overripe bananas "to help out."

But it was much too busy too soon. We hadn't had that slow period of a soft opening that helps a restaurant work out the kinks. We were immediately thrust into the spotlight and expected to deliver. There wasn't enough storage space or prep hours to handle the food our numbers were demanding. I hadn't yet figured out how and when to order meat and fish to keep the freshest supply in our tiny four-by-six-foot step-in refrigerator.

We had back rent to pay, plus we still owed the electrician. So there was no complaining about the attention and the remarkable first week's sales. But as fast and furious as it all came, it died just as abruptly. It was August in DC, a notoriously slow time for any business. And here we were in an upper northwest neighborhood with no other businesses in sight, with so many people still out there who hadn't yet heard of us.

As much as I hated to admit it, those first crazy days of business did not produce our best work. I'm certain we let some customers down with poor service, slow service, and by running out of food. They came to the window by the stove that looked out onto the dining room and told me so. Many of them were trembling, they were so angry. *What kind of restaurant doesn't serve corn bread? How is it that a restaurant could run out of chicken at nine o'clock? What do you mean there's no carry-*

out? Don't you know that Aunt Jemima is not a positive symbol for black people? No alcohol? We're not coming back. You've lost our business. We definitely won't be back. You won't last the year.

By now we were down to a busboy and a couple of servers. Robin worked the dining room most of the week, while Roshena and I were in the back of the house. The dishwashers coming and going and prep cooks never working out didn't matter much because there wasn't much to do for the twenty customers that came each night. When Marcus Drury came every morning with his resume listing years of prepping and baking experience, I was reluctant to hire him. There just wasn't enough money coming in. But the weekends were picking up. On Friday and Saturday nights we needed two servers to work the dining room. I asked Marcus to come in Thursday nights to prep on the little table beside the step-in. He agreed to the one night and as promised, he reported to work on Thursday. Roshena looked at his shoes and sucked air through her teeth. "What you doin' coming to work in a kitchen with dress shoes on?" He looked down at his feet and swayed a bit, catching himself on the handle of the freezer. "I'm perfectly fine in these shoes," he answered her, tying on an apron over a satiny collared shirt. I handed him the book of recipes and showed him where we kept the flour, sugar, salt, vinegars, shallots, and olive oil.

"We need biscuits in the oven by five-thirty and all of the dressings," I explained. "We don't need the dressings tonight, but it will give us a good start tomorrow." Roshena and I went back to cooking for the five people who had made their way to the dining room. They'd surely be ordering the meatloaf. The meatloaf was a safe bet. We weren't selling much seared duck breast. I could hear Marcus in the back thumbing through the pages of the recipe book. He stopped and said, "Meatloaf, oh man!" I went back to the table where he was stationed. The stand mixer was spinning hard and flour was flying out onto the table. He looked up at me, startled. Flour was on his face and down his shirt. He was untying his apron. (A dead give-away: Most cooks wrap the string around and tie it in front. Marcus was fumbling in the back, undoing the novice's blind back tie.) "I didn't think this was going to be all of that." He gestured at the cookbook. Dusting the flour out of his clothes, he headed through the dining room and was gone.

"He was drunk, you know," Roshena said, grabbing the broom. "Tore up from the floor up," she said, giggling.

"Yeah, I know." I turned off the mixer.

Finding reliable staff became our biggest dilemma. One busy night after the article appeared, Richard sat and ate in the dining room with a friend. Robin had been circulating the dining room filling waters and coffees. He stopped her and asked for a job.

"Well, the only thing we need right now is a dishwasher."

"I can start tomorrow," he said, looking at her seriously.

"But . . . you're . . ."

"I'm missing an arm? Yeah, I know." He grabbed the four glasses and two soda bottles with his big, long fingers and lifted them off the table. "My father always told me that I could do whatever I set my mind to." She hired him on the spot.

He was a fine dishwasher. But I was still staying late into the night to sweep and mop the entire kitchen after everyone left.

There were some things he just couldn't do. Like take off the rubber gloves dishwashers wear to dull the heat of the scorching water. He'd just wildly shake his arm until the glove flew off. I was buying them by the case, handing him the one he needed, and stuffing the spare back into the box. At the end of the night he'd yank it loose with his teeth and then whip his arm until the glove flew off. When the call came and he got a job at the parks department he'd been shooting for, he gave his notice. I was finding gloves behind the freezer, underneath the ice machine, and on top of the cooler long after he'd gone.

Robin had designed and printed flyers. The girls spent their summer slipping the half sheets of bond paper touting menu items into mailboxes all over the neighborhood. It was definitely sparking the curiosity of many living nearby. It was good to have Magalee and Sian around with all of our early staffing issues. On opening day my daughters were eight and twelve. Aside from blanketing the area with flyers there wasn't much they could do. Still, I thought it important that they get involved and stay involved. I wanted them to feel part of something big. And if Colorado Kitchen turned out to be a success, they needed to know that they had something to do with it. Sian started by gathering spatulas and slotted spoons for the hot side first thing Sunday morning. Then she cracked ninety eggs into a bucket. Standing on a milk crate, she blended them with cream. Magalee peeled garlic, diced tomatoes, and portioned the butter with a melon baller. When the servers were suddenly swamped we could count on the two to run food to tables or brew coffee on the fly.

There were nights when I didn't have someone beside me making salads. Magalee would close her book, balance one of my chef hats on her head, and tie on an apron. There is not a better classroom than a restaurant. The girls have learned about teamwork and the responsibility of being depended upon. They've done the wrong thing and have had the chef shout at them—Magalee tapped cinnamon instead of powdered sugar on the chocolate tart before sending it out; Sian wanted to wear her Halloween costume nails for one more day and had them on while cracking the eggs for scrambling. It took her most of the morning. She was made to remove the long, fake nails when a customer having a plate of eggs near the end of service found them crunchy with shell fragments. I know that the lessons they've learned from their experiences at the restaurant will stay with them forever. Magalee always looks before she sprinkles and Sian has sworn off fake nails. I am convinced there are some things better learned in the stressful environment of a restaurant kitchen.

I'm always learning. And I've never forgotten the lessons I learned when I first started working. I remember finally feeling comfortable at the grill at my first real cooking job at the Morrison-Clark Inn. I had become relaxed and confident. I looked forward to work. It had become easy for me. Then there was the day I came in to find the cooler at my station empty. There weren't even any chopped chives for garnish. I had to make everything—every sauce, every side, every starch. José had worked the station the night before and left me with no *mise en place* (all the components to make the items on the menu that come from my side of the line).

I had to make the lentil dhal for the salmon as well as the

accompanying tomato chutney. I had to reduce the chicken stock with rosemary for the roasted chicken sauce. I had to blanch green beans and zucchini and cook pasta. Then I had to pluck the wilting leaves of mint for the lamb au jus and blend mustard and Scotch for the tenderloin sauce. After all of that I had to peel roasted peppers for the roasted pepper aioli that went under the grilled halibut. I was panicked that I'd never finish by our six o'clock opening and noticed Chef Susan Lindeborg glancing at me while I was peeling fava beans.

"You okay over there?"

"José left me nothing." I'm sure I was panting, my heart in my throat.

"Oh, good," Chef said, trying not to smile. "I love fresh *mise en place*."

Had she told José to toss everything at the end of the night? I had been humming and whistling and slowly sipping from my pitcher of cola from three o'clock to six. Now I was running around and sweating. It worked. The next time I was confronted with an empty fridge, I dug in and didn't look up or complain until my cooler was full and there was enough sauce and chutney for José's next shift.

There were days when I had to make all of the sauces, help with the salad dressings, and make family meal or the soup of the day. Susan and José had forced me to be responsible—to be a better cook and a more valuable kitchen citizen. I was now able to prepare my station, help another cook, and do other chores in the kitchen. They had made me stronger.

Susan had watched me go from a panic-stricken beginner to a competent rookie who had settled into a comfortable routine—so long as the rest of the staff carried me. And it was that attitude that stood between me and a successful cooking career. Well, it had been about a year and I wasn't new any-more. I was coasting at the grill. Susan and José noticed.

I first witnessed the "coasting" phenomenon when I was chef at Broad Street Grill. There was the training week. And then there were the tense first few weeks we were open, so I noticed when my staff took to coasting. There was an audible sigh in the kitchen one night. This comes only after a few weeks of panic. On opening night, the sauté cook, the man at the grill, and the woman working the salad station all had that knot of worry in their brow. After they'd had a few successful nights putting out decent food, the worry lines went away and they smiled every once in a while. They'd duck and laugh it off when the fryer spit back at them or started, jumped, and finally giggled when the hot pot handle worked its way between the buttons of a chef coat.

But on the first really busy night, the one where they haven't stopped moving for a second—when cooking on the line is more like filling a mesh sack with sand—the panic sets in again. Confidence comes from surviving those nights and, eventually, taking them in stride.

As a chef you look forward to the day that your staff gets it and is making your food on both slow and busy nights without stress. However, a staff can get too relaxed. The tight standards of a menu they've struggled to learn become as choking as a necktie—and they loosen it the minute they enter the kitchen. The food that once challenged them and begged them to dig deep within themselves just to make it through the night is nothing special—and it shows in careless plates and sloppy *mise en place*. The chef watches helplessly as the staff that was once sharp and disciplined as new recruits turns into pimple-faced, rebellious teens who won't turn off their iPods.

These are the times both chef and parent find it difficult to be heard or heeded. We often repeat ourselves. I reserved raising my voice to the third time I had to tell a cook the same thing I had told him last night or the night before. The fourth time, when I could, I'd let him fall.

"Hey, Mario, don't put so much chutney on the plate. You only need a little."

"Okay, Chef."

"I just made that chutney this afternoon and you've just about used it all."

"Sorry, Chef."

The second time:

"Mario."

"Yes, Chef."

"That's way too much chutney. Here, use this teaspoon instead of a ladle."

Third time:

"Okay Mario, where's the teaspoon for the chutney? You're using a ladle."

"Sorry, Chef."

By now I've realized that Mario isn't listening. He's decided he is going to do it his way. He sees the plate with a generous mound of chutney. Not a horrible thing as far as taste is concerned, but it wobbles the food cost of the plate. When a cook puts too much radicchio, a bitter leaf in the chicory family, in the salad blend, I make him eat it and tell me if it really should be his way. In the case of the chutney, I let Mario run out of it.

"Hey, Chef, is this all the chutney?" It's 6:30 and Mario is scraping the bottom of the container with his ladle. I hand him the recipe book and go back to my station. I usually let them fall when I'm in a position to be of little or no help. I'm in the weeds myself making salads. It's customary in just about every restaurant in the country to run out of a complicated part of your *mise en place* in the middle of a rush. So while orders are flying out of the kitchen printer and I'm busy making salads and working the fryer, Mario has to put up menu items from the sauté station at the same time he's making the mango chutney that goes with our most popular appetizer—the crab cakes.

Fear and panic can be healthy things. While I pull on a fresh pair of gloves and toss the leaves of baby spinach with the roasted garlic dressing, I pretend not to be watching Mario. He's got one eye on the tickets mounting on his side of the line, and the other on the ten mangoes he's got to peel and dice.

Although at that moment Mario might not have agreed, I had no doubt he'd be able to make that chutney in time for the eight orders of crab cakes he had hanging. He's a talented cook. Maybe table six will wait five minutes longer for their seared tenderloin. But now Mario uses a teaspoon and places a delicate amount of chutney between two perfectly browned crab cakes. He also had the gift of a little panic that night to build his confidence. He'll run out of chutney again and it will be no big deal. The biggest lesson learned, however, is that I'm not always going to give him all the chutney he needs to cover his lapses in judgment.

I've found that my kids and my cooks often learn best after they've ignored my warnings and painted themselves into a corner. Repeating myself does nothing for them. I may bite my tongue to keep from saying "I told you so," but there is nothing more valuable than the hard-earned lesson they get when I let them fall.

There have been times Magalee has fallen and I've had nothing to do with it. It is this wicked combination of stubbornness, naïveté, and often uncurbed enthusiasm that leads her to go places without even asking my opinion (or heeding my warnings). Sometimes I'm just way too busy and simply catch the change in lighting or a shift of shadow just as she passes in front of a light fixture on her way down. Then: Boom!

"Are you okay, honey?" I ask carefully. I know it's bad when I've got to reach for the crowbar and pry it out of her. Between crying hiccups she manages to admit that she went ahead and did something I advised against. More often what has Magalee heading for the linoleum are the usual sources of angst that become life-and-death issues for a teenager. She confessed a crush and now the whole school knows about it. Or the class clown intercepted a note she was passing and read it aloud in the cafeteria.

My oldest daughter was never much for dolls and tea sets. She treasured the unusual gifts that appeared under the Christmas tree or in the pile on her birthday. One year the Ouija board kept her attention all day. Then there was the book of spells that had her memorizing incantations and burning candles. When I saw the tarot card set complete with fully illustrated analysis and interpretation guide at the bookstore, I had a feeling Magalee would like it. I had no idea that she would study tarot and learn the cards and readings better than she would her schoolwork.

Soon she was telling everyone's fortune. She advised the busboy that continuing on his current path meant trouble. She counseled a server that he needed to follow his heart and pursue a career in dance, despite having pulled the card where a man is sprawled on the beach facedown, his back a pincushion of spears—this just meant there would be difficult times ahead. She was good, however, at stressing that every card had a positive and negative side. Even the dreaded death card hinted at renewal.

Magalee carried those tarot cards with her everywhere. She shuffled in the restaurant sitting by herself at table thirteen. In the car I could hear them flipping off of her thumb and slapping against each other, no longer having to look in the rearview mirror to see that she was giving herself a reading, the cards balancing on her knees. I had to step in, however, when she twisted a hair band around the fraying deck and stuffed it into her book bag.

"You're not taking those to school, are you?" I asked, well aware that the response would be accompanied by a rolling-eyed, pleading glance heavenward.

"Yes . . . I promised Amanda I'd give her a reading."

"You promised? Meaning you've been talking about this at school."

"Of course, Mommy," she said, matter-of-factly, pouring a glass of milk. "All my friends know that I do tarot and that I'm a witch."

"Okay, *Esmeralda,* I strongly suggest you not do readings for your friends at school." I'm trying to imagine how she worked witchcraft into cafeteria conversation. Here was one of those times when whether I shouted it, said it, or sang it, my junior witch was going to her Catholic high school with a dog-eared set of tarot cards despite my admonishments and warnings. This would have to be one of those times that I let her see for herself. Let her feel the repercussions without me shielding her when flippant declarations of witchcraft ricochet around a school that has a chapel beside the main office.

Magalee has nothing but confidence in me. She is certain how I feel about her—no worries there. This often means I get the short end of the stick. It is more often her friends she tries hard to please and impress. So when her God-fearing associates expressed their dismay at the notion of a schoolmate practicing witchcraft, she quickly toned down the Samantha Stephens rhetoric and quietly slipped those cards into her backpack.

Children are changing beings. What held their interest like superglue one day stays on as well as a Post-it note the next. Magalee no longer took those cards with her everywhere. Her younger sister reached the point in her life where she found the mirror more entertaining than the television. At first she locked herself in the bathroom and had to stand on the toilet to stave off a bad hair day. Then she resorted to the mirror in an old compact to get her bangs just right or to smear on the fifth coating of lip gloss. Sian, finally happy with her appearance, would hum or sing in the car while I sped through yellow lights, came to a slight pause at the stop sign, and frantically searched maps for shorter and shorter cuts so she would make it to school on time.

By the time I got to work and was about to begin my stressful day at the restaurant I felt as if I'd already been through a busy Friday night. I had to get the stress out of my life and make Sian accountable for her own timing in the morning. She hadn't a care in the world getting to school while I risked life, limb, and points on my driver's license to make up for the time lost to Sian's pillow punching and primping. Bright and early Monday morning I walked Sian to the Metro bus stop. I gave her bus fare and explained that if she got on the H2 every day by 7:20 she'd arrive at school on time. Sian wasn't too happy about taking the bus by herself. In fact, she was late to school four or five times. But she got it, eventually. Today, she grabs a paper and rides like the rest of the commuters. And my blood pressure is back to normal.

Sian became an expert in traversing the city using public transportation. But she found the walk from our house to the bus stop unbearable. Rollerblades would get her to the bus stop in half the time, she claimed. Sian would not listen when I told her it was a bad idea. Downhill, just beyond a complicated four-way intersection, this was a bus stop one should walk to. Sian was a stubborn little girl. I got up early with her so she could see for herself. She had it all figured out. She'd carry her change of shoes in her backpack and roll her leggings up and stow them in her helmet once she got on the bus. I followed closely behind her and held my breath when we got closer to that intersection. Children's Hospital was on the other side of the overpass. I figured I could carry her there if I had to. Traffic was light this early, but as we got closer to the intersection the hill made it difficult for Sian to control her speed. She was way ahead of me now and when I shouted Stop! and she didn't, I knew she was out of control. She had to wrap herself around a lamppost to keep from skating into the passenger door of a yielding Buick. Sian still objects when I say no. And she ardently argues her case no matter how often I give her the opportunity to prove things to herself. I'll continue to remind her of her skating fiasco until she develops an ombudsman of her own.

"And thy commandment all alone shall live within the book and volume of my brain," Hamlet promised his dead father. But even he was unable to deliver. Over the years as chef and mother, I've found that yelling, screaming, and threatening do little to get staff or children to listen. You can warn and counsel. If they are bent on doing it their way, a firm hand at times has the opposite effect. But the best lessons—the ones that stay with them—are those they learn themselves. Nothing speaks louder than the "hard way" or "just enough rope."

MANGO CHUTNEY

Mangoes are always available at Latin markets.
Be sure to get the roundest ones you can find.
A ripe mango should yield slightly under the pressure
of a gentle squeeze. It should also smell sweet.

MAKES ABOUT 3 CUPS

1 RED ONION, DICED

1/2 CUP LIGHT BROWN SUGAR, PACKED

1/4 CUP SHERRY VINEGAR

4 MANGOES, PEELED AND DICED INTO 1/2-INCH CUBES

1 JALAPEÑO PEPPER, SEEDS REMOVED, FINELY DICED

SALT AND PEPPER

In a small saucepan bring the onions, brown sugar, and vinegar to a boil. Lower the heat and simmer until the mixture is reduced by one-third and starts to thicken. Let it cool. Pour over the diced mangoes and mix in the diced jalapeño. Season with salt and pepper to taste. Store refrigerated in a tight-lidded plastic container.

Eleven

FROM THE LEMONS, THERE'S GREAT LEMONADE

And the bathrooms are over there." Magalee slapped the menus down and turned abruptly to the next couple at the door. I couldn't help but notice from my kitchen window the puzzled expressions on the faces of the folks sitting down.

"Magalee," I asked when she had seated the last table, "why are you telling everyone where the bathroom is when you seat them?" She was nervous, so I asked gently.

"That's what everyone always asks me when I'm in the dining room," she answered in a quivering voice and headed for the door with menus in her hand. Magalee wasn't the only one that Colorado Kitchen pushed out of their comfort zone. In those first months customers from other neighborhoods would call first and ask, "Will my car be safe?" They walked briskly to the door and were reluctant to linger in the dining room when the sun went down. Colorado Avenue did have its share of street characters. From across the street they sat on milk crates and socialized over 40 cans of beer in paper bags. A gentleman who walked the block from dawn to dusk wearing a Superman T-shirt under a sport coat suffered from Vietnam War–induced dementia. Superman had enough left from his pension check one day to come in for an ice cream soda. Other than that, none of the milk crate crowd ever darkened our door. If a menu item required one of us to go to the liquor store across the street for a bottle of Bacardi or E&J Brandy (Easy Jesus as Roshena called it) the guys on milk crates would invade our personal space and insist that the purchase be shared. But they were harmless. There were times when a drunk we didn't recognize stumbled through the door. Robin and I would come from behind the stove or the register and physically toss the offender out. This was a line drawn deep. We couldn't let our guard down on this front. Word always had a way of getting out. As far as the neighborhood was concerned, we were not to be messed with.

The dark circles and frantic look in our eyes certainly contributed to the image. We'd hoped for a change for the better when the heat of August gave way to cooler September. But it was October and we were still way below what we needed to pay the bills. I put off cashing my paycheck week after week.

"We're going down," Robin said one evening. It became her nightly mantra. A few couples and families from the neighborhood had become our regulars. A couple of hours into the dinner service they'd put us to work. When they'd leave we were left to look at each other in the quiet of the dining room. "We are so going down," she'd say again. I was worried, too, but I held out hope. I had been at this lonely dining-room place before. Weeks after Cashion's and Evening Star opened there were so many nights we waited and waited, until the reviews came out. I knew that all we needed was to get the word out. The girls were in school. When they were done with their homework and while it was still daylight, they were again given the small stack of flyers to slip into nearby mailboxes.

But we were still just a curiosity. When flyers lured nearby residents in, they could see that we had created a place where prices and variety made it easy to eat at Colorado Kitchen as often as twice a week. Although I changed what we offered from the kitchen every four weeks, it was a simple enough repertoire for me to prep and cook on my own. This way I could handle the no-shows and call outs. In the past, owners heaped big menus on me with added items so that everyone would be pleased. As far as I was concerned, there was no use casting so wide a net. I had long given up trying to please everyone. The menu had to represent what I felt was important to express with food and what fit with what Colorado Kitchen stood for—uplifting, classic American cuisine. Customers had to be willing to go along for the ride with me driving. Each plate was an edible example of my philosophy of a commercial kitchen's function.

Maybe I lacked confidence in this philosophy when we first opened; I worried that few would be willing to pay top dollar for what Colorado Kitchen stood for. So we opened with food prices well below market. I viewed the low prices as an incentive to try us. I wasn't 100-percent convinced that people would be willing to try my food without that incentive.

One of the flyers invited neighbors to come for Burger Night. Over the years, I had developed a recipe for an outstanding burger. We added interest by making the burger exclusive to Thursday nights, lunch on Fridays, and dinner on

Sundays. Not only was it an inexpensive way to get people in the door, but I also looked at our burger as a way to correct what I saw as a food trend away from the simplest forms of American food. I believe an American restaurant has to have a good burger. The suggestion to add it to the menu at Evening Star, as well as my old boss Susan Lindeborg's unabashed declaration of the splendor of a good burger, led me to study burger art. I used the Lipton soup mix theory (seasoning with garlic and onion) and came pretty close to perfection at Broad Street Grill. And it became the basis for a juicier, more tender execution of burgers at Colorado Kitchen. The eight-ounce Angus burger, studded with roasted garlic and minced onion, was an instant hit. During a slow Friday lunch, it opened *Washington Post* food critic Tom Sietsema's eyes and he instantly understood what I was trying to do.

When it appeared in the *Washington Post Magazine* in November, his review led with the burger and offered glowing praise for almost every menu item—from the eggs Benedict to the chicken wings. Suddenly my little restaurant in upper Northwest was on every DC foodie's radar.

The glowing description of Colorado Kitchen shined a spotlight on our humble store. People started coming from all over and the distance didn't stop them from becoming regulars. Gwen and her husband came all the way from Centreville. Andrea and Burt brought at least two people with them every Saturday from Alexandria. Kevin and Barbara wanted us to open a store in their Columbia Heights neighborhood. And Pat drove down from Takoma Park. It was a good feeling, becoming so many people's favorite restaurant.

That first review gave us a stamp of legitimacy. We had indeed really arrived and we were staying. We were finally filling the dining room. Paying the back rent and the electrician didn't seem so remote. More attention followed. There were reviews in more papers and magazines, and national coverage. *Fox 5 Morning News* broadcast from the restaurant while I dipped fresh donuts into melted chocolate.

The out-of-the-way location, warm décor, and simple menu created an atmosphere of welcome and made Colorado Kitchen the crossover gathering place of the District. Black, white, Asian, young, old, tattooed cyclist, church lady, heterosexual, homosexual, Republican, Democrat—no one felt excluded. In the dining room on any given Sunday every group was well represented in the fifty seats. Although some of our policies did rub folks the wrong way, it only added to the intrigue. There is no kids' menu at Colorado Kitchen. No grilled cheese, no hot dogs. We have no accommodations for carry-out. In any case, our unorthodox approach had people talking. While the reviews brought them in, it was the quality of the cooking that brought people back again and again.

If you ask Magalee or Sian, they'll tell you I'm pretty good at saying "No." I believe in quality ingredients—in seeking the best produce, the highest-quality beef, the finest chocolate. But I only use them seasonally. No matter how much a customer—even a regular customer—would beg, I did not serve our popular white corn chowder in December. And the crab cakes, we'd run out of them. As delicious as they are, they are available only during the late spring and early summer, when the best blue crabs can be harvested from the Chesapeake Bay. It took discipline as well as marketing savvy. Limited availability is great for sales and helped me to be taken seriously. I gained a reputation as a chef concerned more about presenting the best product than about collecting money for a plate of food. I soon earned a spot as one of the top chefs in town.

I felt vindicated. The icing on the cake was that we were doing it my way and getting great reviews and surpassing sales goals every week. Things were falling into place, better than we had predicted. The story of Colorado Kitchen was featured in national newspapers, magazines, and on the Food Network. Keeping up, making sure we were doing things better than we were doing them before, meant hard work. Robin and I were working harder than we'd ever worked before. As a top dining destination in town we had our work cut out for us.

The pressure was on. There were days and nights where customers waited in a line that roped around the building. For Sunday brunches we geared up to serve over 100 customers. Magalee had started working in the dining room and was now an efficient busboy that the servers counted on to help the day go smoothly. Sian made sure the customers waiting on the sidewalk had coffee if they needed it.

I wish all staff were as reliable. There were days Robin and I worked the line and then hurried back to the dish machine and the pot sink to take care of the dirties. We lost staff to drugs and alcohol, as well as to the law. We tried advertising in the local paper and working with agencies that helped the homeless, immigrants, and the learning disabled.

Eric was sent to us to wash dishes by Father Bond from the employment agency at the men's shelter. He was working out okay until the Sunday he left after his shift and came back un-expectedly, demanding I leave the kitchen to come talk to him.

"What are the terms?" he insisted.

"The terms?" I asked. I had to lean closer to understand him.

"Yes." He was pounding his fist into his big palm. "I need to know the terms of this deal."

Did Father Bond tell Eric that he now owned a restaurant and just needed to wash dishes while he waited for the ownership transfer and to be fitted for top hat and spats?

"Eric," I assured him, "there are no terms. You are the dishwasher. You do not own Colorado Kitchen. You wash dishes four days a week and earn eight dollars an hour." I escorted him out while Robin called Father Bond. I was happy to wash dishes for the rest of the weekend so long as we were rid of Eric.

David was probably the most experienced worker in the dining room on any given night. He didn't speak very much English, but he knew exactly what needed to be done without having to be asked. One Sunday night he emerged from a taxi and came inside.

"Is David working tonight?" I asked. He never worked on Sundays. I was about to ask again. Robin wasn't answering. She and Roshena were staring at David as he swayed a little in his flip-flops. That's when I noticed he wasn't wearing any pants. He was taken down to the basement to sober up. After a few cups of coffee and a sandwich, he was put into a cab and sent home. When he asked about the deduction from his paycheck a week later, Robin reminded him about the incident and showed him the receipt the cab driver had given her. He remembered and later that week returned the old chef pants of mine that he'd borrowed. But it was the stealing that got David removed from the staff. He was caught taking cash off the tables and out of the check presenters. For months we thought we had been victims of the old "dine and ditch." But it had been David all along. We hadn't seen him in almost a year when the U.S. Marshal came to the door. He had a picture of David in a big blue binder. There were misdemeanors and felony charges: assaults, larceny, parole violations. He had jumped bail on his latest charge and they were looking for him. He was considered dangerous. I was glad he was gone.

It has been a challenge to maintain seasoned staff. But now we live by a rule that sometimes means the owners have to dig in. The slightest sign of trouble, the slightest suspicion, the inkling that someone isn't going to work out or will fail to show when we need them most is cause to make an immediate personnel change. There is too much riding on it and each member of the team has to fulfill his duty to expectations. The entire staff knows ultimately where the buck comes to an abrupt halt.

I confessed to an interviewer that there is a certain amount of comfort in working for someone else. An employed chef sleeps better at night knowing a power failure and subsequent spoiling of everything in the cooler doesn't come out of her pocket. As chef and owner there is a lot riding on my shoulders. There are at least ten other people counting on me to produce, innovate, and keep the customers coming. Their paychecks depend upon it. There is payroll to meet and bills to pay. None of that can happen if people aren't coming to pay for the food that comes out of my kitchen. I keep an eye on the bank account and make adjustments to keep those figures as high as I can. This might mean taking an item off the menu if it doesn't meet our food cost parameters.

It's also meant firing some of my favorite people. Patron, as he called himself, came to us from West Africa. Colorado Kitchen was his second job. He spent his days parking cars at a busy garage downtown. He was a handsome guy with a great smile. He didn't mind slicing pound after pound of onions or running into the dining room with me to keep a vagrant from entering the bathroom. He told us he was Muslim and had to pray every evening. During Ramadan I cooked for him at the end of his fast—whatever he wanted. Roshena warned me that I was spoiling him. She took him the heaping plate of fried chicken, shaking her head. "Here, Patron," I heard her say. "And that's all you get. When does this ramalan end anyway, shoot?"

I hated the day that I had to fire Patron. But I had no choice. Roshena was right. I couldn't use the phone because he was on it all day. Then there were times I went to the dish area to talk to him or hand him something and he was nowhere in sight. I would look outside and watch as he hopped onto the bus. It all went bad after that woman came into his life. From what I could understand she was a married office worker from the building downtown. Suddenly he was dressing differently, coming in late and leaving early. He told Roshena that he had to call his wife and he would tell her the words that ended it. Then he would never go back to Africa and his three children.

"What you gonna say?" she asked him. She couldn't believe that a phone call could do so much.

"I have to say, I divorce you," Patron said softly. "I have to say it three times." I didn't sleep that night thinking about what I had to do in the morning. But he had been on the phone and snuck out again that day. I got in early and waited for him. I had his work shoes in a bag. I handed it to him as I told him that he didn't work here anymore.

Every day there seemed to be a test of my intestinal fortitude. I never imagined running a restaurant would be so complex and emotionally demanding. The open kitchen design gave customers easy access to me. I had to control my language, my temper, my sense of humor, and my responses to some of the things customers said to me once they realized that they could do something they'd never been able to do at any other restaurant—speak directly to the chef.

Once, a customer came to my kitchen window. I had trained myself to not show the stress of work on my face when customers came by to talk to me. "I really enjoyed it," he said. He'd had the salmon. I'd watched him eat it. "I had the salmon." He slipped the toothpick in between an incisor and a molar. "It was kind of expensive but it was good."

"I'm sorry, did you say expensive?" I knew he wouldn't be coming back, so I let a hint of irritation seep into my voice. "You've got to be kidding me." Ours were the lowest prices in town. Nowhere could you get an eight-ounce portion of fresh fish with a lemon *beurre blanc* for less than fifteen dollars, and ours was priced at eleven seventy-five. It was no use. To the infrequent diner, or the diner who usually went for fast food, we would always be too expensive.

And maybe that was a good thing. I had to have the guts to raise the prices. Part of my responsibility was raising the prices so that fluctuations in the cost of cream and butter didn't keep me from cashing my paychecks or rewarding staff. I had to start to see the value in my work.

When I was in marketing I put on a designer suit and went

to speak as a panelist at a freelance writers' conference. "Make sure you're paid what you're worth," I remember telling them. "Set your rate and stick to it." I told them they needed to be strong and refuse business from anyone not willing to pay them the standard they'd established for themselves. I was finding it hard to live by my own principles. The cheapskate customer helped me see that there was no reward in being the cheapest restaurant in town. The prices had to accurately reflect the value in our product. I had to believe that my food was worth it. You really can't be in this business if you don't believe that your product is the best out there. I had to believe in myself.

It appears there were enough customers who believed as well. We've been able to attract a great customer base of locals and people who drove thirty or forty miles to eat at Colorado Kitchen. The restaurant's numbers are steadily climbing. We hope to gross a half million in sales. This really can be attributed not only to our strict adherence to what we perceived as our image and purpose—expertly prepared, classic American cuisine in a "grandma's kitchen" atmosphere—but also in our ability to be flexible in how we got there.

After a lot of pressure from customers and food critics, we finally gave in and got a beer and wine license. And it has definitely added a new and different component to the dining experience at Colorado Kitchen. But we refused to waver on the core principles of the restaurant.

It seemed crazy at first. Even our friends in the industry— folks running independent restaurants in town—scratched their heads when we told them where and what Colorado

Kitchen would be. But what seemed crazy—starting a new career in food, working as a chef, and opening a restaurant in the middle of a "nowhere" neighborhood—no longer seems crazy at all. Through it all my daughters have been witness to the rough times and got to watch everything finally turn out alright.

Five years after opening, the restaurant is thriving. And it's been more than twelve years since I started cooking school. When I left marketing, got divorced, and started that job carving carrots at the vineyard, I tossed and turned, wondering how I would provide for my family. That's no longer the biggest concern. Now I struggle over what to cook and serve at the benefit where I'm scheduled to appear, whether we should close down service when the television crew comes in, or which chef coat I should wear for the holiday photo shoot where I'll be posing with chefs I used to read about when I was a young line cook.

It's not all television and glamour shots. There still is a lot of hard work involved, just doing the day-to-day. I still try not to scorch the soup or cut my fingertip off. A hot pot handle still might find its way into my sleeve and burn my elbow.

After four chef jobs in four years, I suppose I had learned how to do this job. Based on the way my resume looked, however, I'm not sure anyone would have hired me. There didn't seem any alternative but to be my own boss. There was no way to avoid the lean times, when I was borrowing from Peter and hiding from Paul. It's not just that given hindsight I can now say that it was the right thing to do, despite the nail-biting and teeth-chattering times. There really was no other way I could have survived in the food business. Colorado Kitchen had to happen and it had to work. Sticking through it all took guts. It helped to be hungry. I don't think I wanted anything more. I didn't step on any necks to get here. However, I would seriously injure anyone looking to damage what I've built. There are times I really had to dig deep and do something I never thought I could do. There's much more than money and time invested in Colorado Kitchen.

Sometimes we have to close our eyes and jump in and face our worst fears. This can take any form. I recall pulling it all together and, in my calmest voice, firing a coked-up dishwasher and making him leave the restaurant. Then there was the night after the review came out when I found myself working the line alone because I'd lost Roshena. She had finally achieved her lifelong dream and was declared disabled. She now got a check every month without having to work for it.

And then there was the cheesecake. I'd avoided making cheesecake in this kitchen. I knew I had run out of excuses when folks asked whether we would ever serve it. I didn't own a springform pan, is what I'd tell people. Until one day when Robin came back from running errands. "Look what I found," she said, smiling. She pulled the gleaming stainless-steel baking pan out of the shopping bag. I had no more excuses. In his review in the *Post Magazine* Tom Sietsema called it "slick and one-dimensional." But the customers loved it. We paired it with a blueberry glaze and it became one of our most popular desserts.

COLORADO CHEESECAKE

*I couldn't help but twitch a little when customers complained
that there was no graham cracker crust. They'd grumble
until they'd get a good forkful in their mouth.*

MAKES 12 SLICES OF CAKE

8 OUNCES CREAM CHEESE

6 OUNCES RICOTTA

GRATED ZEST AND JUICE OF 1 LEMON

1 CUP SUGAR

1 TABLESPOON FLOUR

1/2 TEASPOON SALT

5 EGGS

*In a stand mixer, blend all but the eggs over low speed until
well blended. Add the eggs one at a time. Blend on low speed
after each egg is added, until completely blended. Pour the
batter into a buttered and floured 9-inch springform pan.
Bake for 20 minutes in a 325-degree oven. Reduce the oven
temperature to 250 degrees and bake for another 50 minutes
or until set. Allow the cake to cool completely before remov-
ing from the pan. Serve with blueberry glaze.*

BLUEBERRY GLAZE

*This glaze is great on cheesecake and ice cream,
or over a still warm, freshly baked biscuit.*

MAKES 1 CUP OF SAUCE

1 TABLESPOON PORT OR SHERRY

1 CUP SUGAR

2 PINTS FRESH BLUEBERRIES

Heat all of the ingredients over low heat in a stainless-steel saucepan. When the sauce begins to bubble and thicken and the sugar dissolves, remove it from the stove and allow it to cool.

THE BURGER

It took years to finally hit what has quickly become one of the area's best burgers. My inspiration was Lipton Onion Soup mix and it just grew from there.

MAKES 10 BURGERS

5 POUNDS FRESHLY GROUND 80/20 BEEF CHUCK

1/2 CUP ROASTED GARLIC, PURÉED

1 CUP FINELY DICED ONION

2 TEASPOONS SALT

1 TEASPOON FRESHLY GROUND BLACK PEPPER

Gently combine all the ingredients. Using a ring or patty shaper, press ten 8-ounce burgers into a smooth circle. Do not pack the meat, otherwise it will be tough and take a long time to cook. The meat should be loosely held together into a patty. Heat a seasoned cast-iron griddle plate or pan to very high. Sear the burgers on both sides, turning occasionally until the desired internal temperature is reached. Serve immediately on fresh buns with lettuce, tomato, and sliced onion garnish.

THE CRAB CAKES

Yogurt makes for great crab cakes for those of us who aren't big fans of mayonnaise. Crabmeat is naturally sweet and rich. Yogurt adds a much needed tart counterpoint.

MAKES 10 CRAB CAKES

1 POUND JUMBO LUMP CRABMEAT, CLEANED

1/3 CUP YOGURT

1 TEASPOON FINELY DICED PARSLEY

2 TEASPOONS FINELY DICED SHALLOTS

1 TEASPOON DICED CORNICHONS OR GHERKINS

1 TEASPOON CHOPPED CAPERS

1 TEASPOON SALT

1/2 TEASPOON FRESHLY GROUND BLACK PEPPER

2 CUPS BREAD CRUMBS

OIL FOR FRYING

Gently toss together all the ingredients except the bread crumbs. Shape 2 ounces of the mixture into a round cake and coat with the crumbs. Continue shaping the rest into 2-ounce crab cakes until you've shaped all of the crab cake mixture.

Place each crab cake on a tray and let them set in the refrigerator while you heat the oil in a 9-inch frying pan or skillet.
Brown five cakes at a time so as not to crowd the pan. Keep
warm in the oven and serve immediately.

WHITE CORN CHOWDER

There was a time when I hesitated before ordering an entire case
of corn. But this soup is so popular, in the height of the season
I'll go through two or three cases a week in my tiny kitchen.

MAKES 1 GALLON

25 EARS WHITE CORN

1 TABLESPOON BUTTER

1 CUP FINELY DICED ONION

5 QUARTS WATER

2 TEASPOONS SALT

1/2 TEASPOON FRESHLY GROUND WHITE PEPPER

Carefully cut the kernels from the corn and reserve the cobs.
Heat the butter in a soup pot over medium-low heat. Add the
onions and cook them until they are translucent. Add the corn,
the cobs, and the water. Simmer for 20 minutes, or until the
kernels are tender. With a pair of tongs remove the cobs and discard. In a blender purée the corn mixture. Strain through a
sieve and press as much liquid as you can from the hard fibers
that are left behind in the strainer. Reheat the soup, add the salt
and pepper, and serve.

Epilogue

CLOSING TIME

Sunday brunch is over and there's not much to put away. We've run out of bacon, sausage, and eggs broken for scrambled. After family meal, it doesn't take much to clean up the kitchen. I'm tired though, and move a little slower than usual. It's been a long week. Friday, Saturday, and Sunday are three tough days way too close together. I've been running on an adrenaline high, as well as coffee and energy drinks. Now I'm crashing hard.

The girls are waiting. Magalee offers me a donut left over from family meal. It's covered in crushed almonds and honey. Sian's helped herself to a soda and offers me one. She's not allowed to have soda and candy because of her braces, and by giving me a soda, she's hoping I won't notice the root beer she's drinking. I make her pour it out and get herself a glass of milk before I head downstairs and change out of my work clothes.

It's been five years, so shutting the building down for the evening is pretty routine. The ride home is just as routine and we're at the door before I know it. Magalee complains about her aches from carrying the full bucket of dirty dishes to the back. Sian has plenty to tell us about the folks outside waiting to get in. She poured coffee for a woman watching a store go up nearby. "Colorado Kitchen is finally going to have some competition," the woman said. Sian asks me if I'm worried. No, I tell her. We've always had competition. People drive by plenty of restaurants to wait in line in front of Colorado Kitchen. "They're not waiting out there to see you, Sian." We laugh. "Are you sure?" she asks, smoothing down a stray hair on her head. "I'm only kidding." She elbows her sister, who's giving her the "you're insane" look.

My key is in the door and we're already arguing over the shower. I always win this one. Probably because I smell the worst—like food beginning to spoil and sweat. Even the foyer is starting to smell like me. After we've all had a hot shower and a minute to crack our knuckles, there's a minute or two to catch up on e-mail and return phone calls before we head out to dinner. I rarely cook at home anymore. And Sunday night has become our night to eat out together. Usually at the restaurant the girls eat without me. But Sunday night we argue over what we crave, where we haven't been in a while, and where I feel like driving. "Magalee, when you get your license you can make the final decision."

Over dinner we unwind, talk about the day, the months, school, and the restaurant. My dinner companions are great restaurant critics. Magalee rejects the green beans if they're not fresh. Sian tries the lemonade and the pasta and readily announces if it's acceptable or not. "I don't think they make this ravioli here," she says, sliding it around in the sauce with her fork.

When they were younger they'd insist we go to a restaurant where I was once chef. "I'm not there anymore, honey," I'd explain, "The food isn't going to be like you remember." Now they know where to get good Chinese, the best place for pizza. Together we discover a new favorite Thai place. We bond over my work, over food. It settles us into a comfortable spot and we can talk about anything.

"Are you sure it's two and seven-eighths, Mommy?" Sian asked. She was measuring the coffee and the filter was teeming.

"Yeah . . ." I glanced over my shoulder and saw the grounds fill the filter higher than I remembered. Sian knows that tone of voice and paused, looking at me over her glasses. "Well, no . . . I'm not sure," I confess.

Sian was right. It was one and seven-eighths. I watched her brew the coffee. It was a little bit after 9:30 A.M. so there was plenty of time to fill all of the coffee urns and brew enough coffee for her to have outside for the crowd that would be waiting more than an hour to have brunch at Colorado Kitchen. She poured the water into the top, then watched and waited for the pot to fill with hot coffee. When this all started, Sian wasn't tall enough to reach the top of the coffeemaker. In those days she was called on only when we were all about to go down and there was no one else left to help.

We were without Magalee so far this morning. She had spent the night with a friend. She'd be going to college soon and I supposed Sian would be taking over her duties. Today, I figured I might as well let Sian practice until Mag makes it in. Of course when the door opens and Magalee comes in, slips her card into the time clock, and pulls on her uniform shirt, she asks Sian to step aside. She's very serious about her job getting the dining room ready for brunch. But Sian can't help but stick around. She's full of questions about the rock concert and Magalee's evening at her friend's house. She'll find something to do to help so that she can pepper her sister with questions and find out as much as she can about what sixteen-year-olds do when they are out on a Friday night.

They are totally unaware that I watch and hear everything. Magalee complains about the kids who were smoking, while Sian grabs a wrapped straw. She holds it between her index and middle fingers and puffs on it. The conversation was different years ago when I was at Broad Street Grill. When I had them in the kitchen with me they talked about cartoons and what they wanted for their birthdays. Magalee peeled potatoes. The starch made her itch. So she scraped the speckled skin off the spuds with too-big gloves over her small hands. Meanwhile, Sian stood on a milk crate so she could drop one egg at a time into the *pâte à choux* while it whipped around in the mixer.

As much as cooking took me away from them, with my crazy schedule working nights and weekends, it brought us together. I doubt there are many other parents in this position these days; the truth is I needed my kids. Having their help eased my panic during those days when I found myself alone in a kitchen except for Magalee singing and peeling five potatoes, or Sian asking me what the eggs do and why she can't just put them all in at once. I still worried frantically about the kitchen and how I was going to make it through another Saturday night with a skeleton crew and only my daughters around to help me prep. And when the babysitter came and took them home I worried about my two little girls. Does Sian need braces? Will Magalee need to have a math tutor?

They are too young to remember and I did my best to hide how hard it was. I went through my days without breathing, protecting them so that they didn't worry and could focus on their schoolwork and childhood. I wanted them to be children and enjoy this time in their lives. They didn't seem to notice that to that end, I walked a tightrope. The girls never lost sleep or wrung their hands. They went through their days as if nothing was wrong.

Even if I'd just lost my job, I couldn't furrow my brow for very long. Their smiles and laughter over breakfast were contagious. The unfailing cheerfulness of my daughters may have been ignorance. Perhaps they were simply too young to understand the gravity of our situation when I lost my job, couldn't cash my checks, or there was no support from their father. But it buoyed me. It raised my confidence with the unyielding knowledge that everything was going to turn out because I'd make it so.

It's funny that although they witnessed it, I don't think the girls really understand what it took to get here. Nor do they see the success of Colorado Kitchen as something to marvel at. "Isn't this how it was supposed to happen, Mommy?" I'm sure that's what they'd say if I asked them.

The best part about the success of Colorado Kitchen is that my daughters have been part of it and with me all the way. They spend an enormous amount of time at the restaurant and have become part of the Colorado Kitchen Community, which includes our neighbors on the avenue, the customers, and our staff. It's an exceptionally large extended family. The girls have surrogate fathers in employees who remember their birthdays and drive them to school band concerts. Regular customers make a point of marking the important days in their lives with gifts and cards. As part of the family, my children were there to catch a glimpse when customers' lives unfolded before us. Growing thin, and then wearing a scarf, a regular customer's wife stops joining him for lunch, finally succumbing to cancer. The older couple that took up table five every Sunday night for hours is suddenly MIA. Then she arrives alone, swollen-eyed and awkward by herself at the counter with a book. He appears weeks later with a much younger girl sitting so close to him their knees touch. The gray is mysteriously gone from his hair. They've seen the pair of twenty-somethings come in every Saturday brunch exposing their tattoos with tank tops and midriff shirts. They uncharacteristically arrive on a Wednesday wearing long-sleeve oxford shirts. Her parents are in town. And he's washed his hair for the occasion. In no time it seems she's obviously pregnant. We all don't realize how long it's been, but it's been months. Months lates Magalee is visibly moved as she pushes the high chair to their table.

They've seen a lot. The restaurant is chock-full of life lessons. There is evidence that hard work has its rewards. Often they see that no matter how hard you try, unfortunately you can't please everyone. They've watched me lose my temper. And they've been there during the times when I've set my jaw in the face of biting criticism. They've carried on with their homework as the cameras rolled and sound techs told them to be quiet. Aside from gaining valuable skills in working for their money, they've seen what it takes to be a chef and a business owner. I hope they've learned that good things can happen when you believe that they can.

I didn't always believe. There were times I simply acted out of desperation. Things had to go our way, because they just had to. I wasn't taking no for an answer. And like a bean stalk, Colorado Kitchen grew into something I never imagined. What started out as a little restaurant that could give us a simple living as a neighborhood joint became a citywide sensation with national media coverage.

It's hard to imagine that the chef featured on the Food Network and in that holiday magazine spread, cooking with the industry's heavy hitters, is me. Just the other day I was a struggling prep cook turning vegetables at the vineyard. I suppose if it didn't seem like I was running a marathon, I could have enjoyed the elevator ride. In any event, it's nice to know that without the farm and the family we started out with, we did more than survive.

More gratifying than the hard-earned success is the realization that cooking is ultimately how I found myself. While the family farm idea may have been a good one, it was only an attempt to add cayenne to spoiled meat. When I let go of the easy answers and concentrated on what I really wanted, I let go of trying to make life more tolerable for the alcoholic I was living with. Once food became the focus, I gave up trying to control the uncontrollable. We all have the opportunity to do great things; I do mine with food. I'm glad I was able to find it. I had to go out of my comfort zone to get my gift out of hiding. I had to test myself. I had to be honest.

GILLIAN CLARK

I hope that's one lesson my children have learned from all of this—to persevere honestly. There is no way you can fail if you just be yourself. My children have learned it's liberating and refreshing to be yourself, to do what you love. And for me the end result is a room full of smiling, happy people. Food has brought peace, honesty, and real giving to my life.

It's also brought more attention then I ever had—phone calls, letters, interviews, television appearances. But I'm never permitted to let it go to my head. There is a greater part of the day when no one hangs on my every word and there's no one in the room who's anxious to meet me. I'm often subject to a classic teenage eye roll because I'm not up on the latest pop star news. I get a giggle or two when I pull something burnt out of the oven. To the girls I will always be simply "Mommy."

Index